FINGER-
TIP
JAPANESE

FINGER-TIP JAPANESE

ENJOY JAPAN AS THE JAPANESE DO

by Walter Long

with Kennichi Shimonishi

New York • WEATHERHILL • Tokyo

First edition, 1994

Published by Weatherhill, Inc.
420 Madison Avenue, 15th Floor
New York, N.Y. 10017

Printed in the U.S.A.

Library of Congress Cataloging in Publication Data

Long, Walter.
Fingertip Japanese / by Walter Long, with Kenichi Shimonishi
— 1st ed.
p.   cm.
ISBN 0-8348-0270-8 : $9.95
1. Japanese language — conversation and phrase books —
English.
I Shimonishi, Kenichi. II. Title
PL 539. L66 1993
495.6' 83421 — dc20   93-8280
                                                   CIP

94 95 96 97 98 8 7 6 5 4 3 2 1

Contents

Introduction

About You

This book is for you if you are planning to visit Japan and are determined not to let the language barrier prevent you from enjoying yourself as you would in a country whose language you understand. A curious and adventurous traveler, you are accustomed to interacting with the local people you encounter, but you lack the time or opportunity to study Japanese intensively in preparation for your trip.

You need some help. But you do not wish to plough through grammatical explanations or memorize cumbersome expressions; you do not want a primer in the Japanese language disguised as a phrasebook. You want a brief and accessible list of serviceable words and expressions, a list comprehensible both to yourself and to your Japanese hosts. And you want some background information on etiquette and customs—not an encyclopedic survey of Japanese culture, but brief pointers on what to say and do to put both you and your hosts at ease in typical situations. Providing such a tool is the goal of *Fingertip Japanese*.

About Phrasebooks

Most Japanese phrasebooks seem written by people who either never had to use them or perhaps, having spent years studying the language, have a perverse interest in making communicating with the Japanese seem difficult. Thus we have books advising us to ask *Sumimasen, danshi yō no toire wa doko desuka?*

(Excuse me, where is the men's room?), when one need only say *Toire wa?* (Toilet?). The latter is certainly shorter and easier, and, if there happens to be a separate facility for each sex, we can leave it to the clever Japanese responding to direct us accordingly.

About Fingertip Japanese

The purpose of this book is to help you communicate, not to foist you off as an eloquent speaker of Japanese. The sentences and expressions given are simple and straightforward. Therefore:

Fingertip Japanese is task-oriented, that is, the words and phrases presented are those you will need to get something or get something done, whether extra *wasabi* (a kind of horse radish) on your sushi or a shirt laundered with no starch. These tasks are grouped according to the situations or places in which they would most likely occur, which are listed as page headings. Only active vocabulary is presented for the most part; as long as your request is being acted upon, you do not really need to understand the Japanese verbal response.

The text is also fully bilingual, with expressions clearly presented in both romanized form, so that you can verbalize them, and in Japanese script, so they can be read by Japanese assisting you. If you encounter difficulty making yourself understood, simply use your fingertip——point to the Japanese text for your request. Far from appearing odd, your action will provide a welcome tool that will help your hosts to understand and assist you.

Each of the seven chapters of this book introduces a main topic (traveling, shopping, eating, etc.), under which are grouped related tasks that visitors to Japan may need to accomplish (giving directions to a taxi driver, buying a necktie, making a dinner reservation). The first chapter is a slight exception in that it introduces general expressions (for times, days, dates, amounts) useful for many tasks.

The expressions recommended for accomplishing each task are the most readily understood and simplest possible. If the expression will require modification for a particular situation, a page number is given where appropriate substitutions for the text marked in bold may be found:

> I'd like five of these.   (NUMBERS, p. 19)
> *Kore o **itsutsu** kudasai.*
> これを5つください。

On page 19, you will find the vocabulary to change "five" to "six," "seven," etc.

In addition to useful words and phrases, *Fingertip Japanese* contains abundant "how-to" information for getting along in Japan. Even if you do not attempt a single Japanese utterance, reading the introduction to each chapter and section, as well as the "Fingertips" at the end of each chapter, will make your time spent in Japan much more enjoyable.

About the Japanese Language

Although this book is intended more for those who do *not* plan to learn Japanese, a few general remarks on the language are in order due to its reputation as formidably difficult. It is true that Japanese is a complex language, but many of the reasons for its complexity will not concern users of this book. For example,

Japanese has many levels of politeness, employed according to the position and relationship of the speakers. All words and phrases in *Fingertip Japanese* are expressed in a neutrally polite mode appropriate for use by visitors from abroad. Likewise, differences in wording due to gender will be mitigated through the use of expressions appropriate to both sexes.

Although the Japanese writing system encompasses a complex amalgam of Chinese characters and indigenous syllabaries, users of *Fingertip Japanese* will not be reading Japanese text, but merely pointing to it. The more than ninety percent literacy rate (highest in the world) of the Japanese people will ensure that your message is understood.

About Japanese Pronunciation

One well-meaning phrasebook advises us to say, as we gaze upon the Imperial Palace in Tokyo: *Koh-REH-gah, TEHN-noh toh goh-KAH-zoh-koo noh OH-moh nah oh-SOO-mah-ee dehs KAH?*, meaning, "Is this the main residence for the Emperor and his family?" Aside from the fact that it is fairly logical that the Emperor and his family live in the Imperial Palace, the question is transcribed in a cumbersome and totally fabricated romanization system, making it unlikely that the hapless Japanese it is inflicted upon will ever understand it.

There is really no excuse for this, as a simple and regular romanization system already exists for the transcription of Japanese, the Hepburn system. Moreover, Japanese use this system themselves, in advertising and in street and shop signs, so knowing how to read it is a useful skill. Using this standard system of romanization, the pronunciation of Japanese is fairly easy. You will generally be understood if you pronounce every syllable, giving each equal stress, and sound vowels as follows:

a	as in father
i	as in Bali
u	as in true
e	as in press
o	as in colt

Romanized Japanese does have one unusual diacritical mark, called a macron, which appears over vowels (for example, ō), and indicates that the vowel should be voiced for twice as long as an ordinary vowel. (Rather than making use of the cumbersome macron, some texts add an "h" after the vowel. The business district of Otemachi, for example, is also written Ohtemachi.) Moreover, because of the typographical problem of putting macron over an "i," this letter is often instead simply doubled, the method used in this book.

About the Japanese

Although adhering to rules of etiquette and behavior that can appear overly rigid to outsiders, Japanese are nonetheless delightfully easy to get along with. According to conventional wisdom, this is for two main reasons: Japanese place great emphasis on tranquility and the appearance of cordiality in interpersonal relationships, and they do not expect non-Japanese to act, or even be able to act, according to their rules.

This latter is occasionally a source of irritation for those who, after studying the Japanese language and culture for many years, are still asked if they can use chopsticks. For others, however, the innate politeness and cultural chauvinism of the Japanese are distinct advantages. Japanese are proud of their nation and its accomplishments, and will go to great lengths to ensure that your stay is pleasant and that you leave with a good impression. Moreover, the cultural pride of the Japanese does not, as in some countries, manifest itself in intolerance toward outsiders who attempt to speak their language. On the contrary, secure in the conviction that non-Japanese can never master it, Japanese welcome the attempts of outsiders to use Japanese, and are delighted to act as tutors.

Thus, if you are simply courteous and considerate you will get along fine, and if you manage to interject an occasional comment or polite expression in Japanese, your reception will be even warmer. Even though you are for all practical purposes a functional illiterate, the Japanese will make sure you get what you want or to where you are going. Although a few do's and dont's are presented throughout the text, chief among them is simply: do relax and have a good time, and don't worry.

FINGER-TIP

TIP

JAPANESE

Getting Started

To interact at all with Japanese *in* Japanese, you will need the expressions in this chapter. Basically, they are of two types: the greetings and responses required for daily use; and the "nuts and bolts" terms you will need to specify types, quantities, times, days, dates, and amounts. These latter appear in list form and the lists will be referred to frequently.

Essential Expressions

As would be expected in a land where *wa* (harmony) is the highest ideal, the "magic words" of our childhood, "please," "thank you," and "excuse me," have their Japanese equivalents, and these are employed with great frequency. They are used so often, in fact, that their meanings have broadened to the point that several of them might be apropriate in a particular situation. Listening to conversations between Japanese will give you a better idea how they are used.

onegai shimasu おねがいします This common equivalent of "please" literally means "I request that you . . ." and is a polite addition to any request for assistance. It can be affixed to a noun, as in *Kōhii onegaishimau* ("Coffee, please"), or stand alone, to get someone's attention, for example, at the front desk of a hotel.

dōzo どうぞ Another "Please," this expression functions as in "Please go right ahead," when indicating that someone should go ahead of you eating, drinking, sitting down, etc.

dōzo yoroshiku どうぞよろしく Literally "Please be good to me," this expression is used when meeting people for the first time, and functions as the equivalent of "Pleased to meet you." Another expression, *hajimemashite*, literally comments "We're meeting for the first time," and is often followed by *dōzo yoroshiku* to form a complete, formal expression used on the important occasion of a first meeting. However, this makes a mouthful for the non speaker of Japanese, and either expression alone is sufficient.

arigatō ありがとう This can be roughly considered "Thanks," the short form of *dōmo arigatō*, by analogy, "Thank you very much." Unless you have won the lottery, the still more formal and longer form, *dōmo arigatō gozaimashita* is really not required.

sumimasen すみません Meaning, "Excuse me," this expression works both as an actual apology (equivalent to *gomenasai*, "I'm sorry"), used when pushing onto a crowded subway, for example, and also overlaps with the meaning of *onegai shimasu*, used when bothering someone for a favor.

dōmo Perhaps the most versatile word in the Japanese lexicon, this literally means "very much," and is used to intensify expressions such as "thank you" (*dōmo arigatō*) and "excuse me" (*dōmo sumimasen*). It has somehow come to be able to stand for the expressions it intensifies; thus you will hear Japanese rapidly saying *dōmo, dōmo, dōmo* to express thanks, *dōmo* for "Hello" to a visitor ("Thanks for coming to see me") and even *dōmo* for "Goodbye" at the end of the work day ("Thanks for a all your efforts").

Tips on using some of the expressions below are given in the introduction to this chapter.

Yes.
Hai.
はい。

No.
Iie.
いいえ。

Thank you.
Arigatō.
ありがとう。

You're welcome.
Dō itashimashite.
どういたしまして。

Please.   (When requesting)
Onegai shimasu.
おねがいします。

Excuse me.   (Getting attention)
Sumimasen.
すみません。

Excuse me.   (Apologizing)
Gomenasai.
ごめんなさい。

That's so, isn't it.   (Expressing agreement)
Sō, desune.
そうですね。

Really?   (Expressing surprise)
Honto?
ほんと？

The English expressions listed here are equivalent rather than exact translations. *Konnichiwa*, for example, literally means "Today is...?" with an implication something like the colloquial English "How's it going today?"

Good morning.
Ohayō.
おはよう。

Good day.
Konnichiwa.
こんにちは。

Good night
Konbanwa.
こんばんは。

How are you?　　　　　　　(Literally, "Healthy?")
Genki desuka?
元気ですか？

Fine, thanks.　　　　　　　(Response to above)
Hai, okagesamade.
はい、おかげさまで。

Pleased to meet you.　　　　(Upon first meeting)
Hajimemashite.
はじめまして。

See you later.　　　(When parting for a short time)
Mata, ne.
またね。

Goodbye.　　　　(When parting for a longer time)
Sayonara.
さよなら。

Although fairly regular, Japanese numbers may seem complex because there are two sets of cardinal numbers from one to ten. The first is used when numbers are stated, as in a phone number or address:

My room number is six.
Heya bangō wa roku desu.
部屋番号は6です。

My extension is 501.
Naisen wa go-zero-ichi desu.
内線は5-6-1です。

It's now 7:00.
*Ima **shichiji** desu.*
今7時です。

0	*rei* (or *zero*)	0
1	*ichi*	一
2	*ni*	二
3	*san*	三
4	*shi* (or *yon*)	四
5	*go*	五
6	*roku*	六
7	*shichi* (or *nana*)	七
8	*hachi*	八
9	*kyū* (or *ku*)	九
10	*jū*	十

The second set of ordinal numbers functions as a general "counter," to specify quantities of something. Although characters for the numbers are given here, Japanese often use Arabic numerals, especially for large numbers, and all Japanese can read them.

I'd like five of these.
Kore o itsutsu kudasai.
これを5つください。

Just one, please.
Hitotsu dake onegaishimasu.
1つだけおねがいします。

Please give me six apples.
*Ringo o **muttsu** kudasai.*
りんごを6つください。

1	*hitotsu*	一
2	*futatsu*	二
3	*mittsu*	三
4	*yottsu*	四
5	*itsutsu*	五
6	*muttsu*	六
7	*nanatsu*	七
8	*yattsu*	八
9	*kokonotsu*	九
10	*tō*	十

Larger numbers follow the regular pattern of Arabic numerals: 2,576, for example is *nisen gohyaku nanajū roku*, literally: "two thousands, five hundreds, seven tens, and six."

11	*jūichi*	十一
12	*jūni*	十二
13	*jūsan*	十三
14	*jūyon*	十四
15	*jūgo*	十五
16	*jūroku*	十六
17	*jūnana*	十七
18	*jūhachi*	十八
19	*jūkyū*	十九
20	*nijū*	二十
21	*nijū ichi*	二十一
22	*nijū ni*	二十二
23	*nijū san*	二十三
30	*sanjū*	三十
31	*sanjū ichi*	三十一
32	*sanjū ni*	三十二
40	*yonjū*	四十
50	*gojū*	五十
60	*rokujū*	六十
70	*nanajū*	七十
80	*hachijū*	八十
90	*kyūjū*	九十
97	*kyūjū nana*	九十七
98	*kyūjū hachi*	九十八
99	*kyūjū kyū*	九十九

Notice that 10,000 is the base amount for the larger numbers; 1,000,000, for example, is expressed *hyaku-man*, or "a hundred ten thousands." Also note the slight pronunciation changes when *hyaku* is linked to 3, 6, and 8 *(sanbyaku, roppyaku, happyaku)*.

100	*hyaku*	百
101	*hyaku ichi*	百一
102	*hyaku ni*	百二
110	*hyaku jū*	百十
111	*hyaku jūichi*	百十一
112	*hyaku jūni*	百十二
121	*hyakunijūichi*	百二十一
130	*hyakusanjū*	百三十
140	*hyakuyonjū*	百四十
200	*nihyaku*	二百
300	*sambyaku*	三百
400	*yonhyaku*	四百
500	*gohyaku*	五百
600	*roppyaku*	六百
700	*nanahyaku*	七百
800	*happyaku*	八百
900	*kyūhyaku*	九百
1,000	*sen*	千
2,000	*nisen*	二千
10,000	*ichiman*	一万
100,000	*jūman*	十万
1,000,000	*hyakuman*	百万
10,000,000	*senman*	千万
100,000,000	*ichioku*	一億

As other Asian languages, Japanese uses "counters," special words combined with the numbers and used to enumerate different types of objects. (One night is counted *ippaku*; one dog, *ippiki*, etc.) In fact, however, you can get along with a few of the most common counters.

I'd like to make a reservation for three.
San'nin no yoyaku o onegaishimasu.
3人の予約をお願いします。

There will be eight people at the meeting.
Hachinin ga sono kaigi ni shusseki suru yotei desu.
8人がその会議に出席する予定です。

General Counter		People		Small Things	
1	*hitotsu*	一	*hitori*	一人	*ikko*	一個
2	*futatsu*	二	*futari*	二人	*niko*	二個
3	*mitsu*	三	*san'nin*	三人	*sanko*	三個
4	*yottsu*	四	*yonin*	四人	*yonko*	四個
5	*itsutsu*	五	*gonin*	五人	*goko*	五個
6	*muttsu*	六	*rokunin*	六人	*rokko*	六個
7	*nanatsu*	七	*shichinin*	七人	*nanako*	七個
8	*yatsu*	八	*hachinin*	八人	*hakko*	八個
9	*kokonotsu*	九	*kyūnin*	九人	*kyūko*	九個
10	*tō*	十	*jūnin*	十人	*jukko*	十個

"Small things" here might be apples, boxes, etc.; "flat things" include stamps and pieces of paper; while "thin things" includes pencils and beer bottles. However, if you cannot recall these common counters, simply use the "general counter" and you should be understood.

These three suitcases are his.
Kono sanko no sūtsu kēsu wa kare no desu.
この3このスーツケースは彼のです。

Let me have two of those melons.
Meron o niko kudasai.
メロンを2こください。

	Flat Things		Long Things	
1	*ichimai*	一枚	*ippon*	一本
2	*nimai*	二枚	*nibon*	二本
3	*sanmai*	三枚	*sanbon*	三本
4	*yonmai*	四枚	*yonbon*	四本
5	*gomai*	五枚	*gobon*	五本
6	*rokumai*	六枚	*roppon*	六本
7	*nanamai*	七枚	*nanabon*	七本
8	*hachimai*	八枚	*happon*	八本
9	*kyūmai*	九枚	*kyūbon*	九本
10	*jūmai*	十枚	*juppon*	十本

As a tourist or visitor to Japan, the item you will likely most often be counting is money. The basic unit of Japanese currency is the yen, which may be roughly equated with a penny. Combine the numbers learned on pp. 18--21 with *yen* (pronounced *'en* following numbers) to form amounts of money.

How much is it?
Ikura desuka?
いくらですか？

It's 2,300 yen.
Nisen sambayku'en *desu.*
2,300円です。

100 yen	*hyaku'en*
210 yen	*nihyaku jū'en*
650 yen	*roppyaku gojū'en*
1000 yen	*sen'en*
2500 yen	*nisen gohyaku'en*
3,870 yen	*sanzen happyaku nanajū'en*
10,000 yen	*ichiman'en*
22,900 yen	*niman nisen kyūhyaku'en*
55,000 yen	*goman gosen'en*
120,000 yen	*jūniman'en*
500,000 yen	*gojūman'en*
3,200,00 yen	*sambyaku nijūman'en*

How many yen to the dollar?
Ichi doru wa nan'en desuka?
1ドルは何円ですか？

As in English, Japanese time expressions can appear in various positions in sentences. For emphasis, they may be placed at the beginning.

Tomorrow we're going to Europe.
Ashita Yōroppa e ikimasu.
明日ヨーロッパへ行きます。

this week	*konshū*	今週
this month	*kongetsu*	今月
this year	*kotoshi*	今年
today	*kyō*	今日
next week	*raishu*	来週
next month	*raigetsu*	来月
next year	*rainen*	来年

Yesterday we went to Kyoto.
Kino Kyoto e ikimashita.
昨日京都へ行きました。

last week	*senshū*	先週
last month	*sengetsu*	先月
last year	*kyonen*	去年

They're coming this morning.
Kesa kimasu.
今朝来ます。

afternoon	*gogo*	午後
evening	*yoru*	夜
tomorrow morning	*ashita no asa*	明日の朝
tomorrow afternoon	*ashita no gogo*	明日の午後
tomorrow evening	*ashita no yoru*	明日の夜

Hours are expressed using the numbers learned on p. 18 plus *ji*. This can be preceded by *gozen* to indicate a.m., *gogo* for p.m.

It's now ten o'clock.
Ima jūji desu.
今10時です。

The train leaves at three this afternoon.
Ressha wa kyō no gogo sanji ni demasu.
列車は今日の午後3時に出ます。

The meeting is tomorrow morning at 8:00.
Kaigi wa ashita no asa hachiji desu.
会議は明日の朝8時です。

1:00	*ichiji*
2:00	*niji*
3:00	*sanji*
4:00	*yoji*
5:00	*goji*
6:00	*rokuji*
7:00	*shichiji*
8:00	*hachiji*
9:00	*kuji*
10:00	*jūji*
11:00	*jūichiji*
12:00	*jūniji*

To the hours on the facing page, add the minutes, or
fun. Note again the slight pronunciation shifts that
occur when this word is added to certain numbers.

It's now 10:20.
*Ima **jūji nijuppun** desu.*
今10時20分です。

The train leaves at 3:35 this afternoon.
*Ressha wa kyō no gogo **sanji sanjūgofun** ni
demasu.*
列車は今日の午後3時35分に出ます。

The meeting is tomorrow morning at 8:30.
*Kaigi wa ashita no asa **hachiji han** desu.*
会議は明日の朝8時半です。

:05	*gofun*
:10	*juppun*
:15	*jūgofun*
:20	*nijuppun*
:25	*nijūgofun*
:30	*han* (or *sanjuppun*)
:35	*sanjūgofun*
:40	*yonjūppun*
:45	*yonjūgofun*
:50	*gojuppun*
:55	*gojūgofun*

The written forms for Japanese days of the week are
picturesquely indicated by the characters for sun,
moon, and the "five elements" of traditional alchemi-
cal theory (fire, water, wood, metal, and earth).

Yesterday was Sunday.
Kinō wa nichiyō(bi) deshita.
昨日は日曜（日）でした。

Today is Monday.
Kyō wa getsuyō(bi) desu.
今日は月曜（日）です。

Tomorrow is Tuesday.
Ashita wa kayō(bi) desu.
明日は火曜（日）です。

Will you be free on Wednesday?
Suiyō(bi) wa hima desuka?
水曜（日）は暇ですか？

Thursday is a holiday.
Mokuyō(bi) wa yasumi desu.
木曜（日）は休みです。

Let's get together Friday night.
Kinyō(bi) no yoru ni aimashō.
金曜（日）の夜に会いましょう。

Saturday is the tenth.
Doyō(bi) wa tōka desu.
土曜（日）は10日です。

The months of the year are easily formed by combining the numbers on p. 18 with the word *gatsu*, meaning "month."

I'm taking vacation in August.
Hachigatsu ni bakēshon o torimasu.
8月にバケーションを取ります。

The weather in Japan is great in October.
Jūgatsu no Nihon no tenki wa subarasii.
10月の日本の天気はすばらしい。

The rainy season starts in June.
*Tsuyu wa **rokugatsu** ni hajimarimasu.*
梅雨は6月に始まります。

January	*ichigatsu*	1月
February	*nigatsu*	2月
March	*sangatsu*	3月
April	*shigatsu*	4月
May	*gogatsu*	5月
June	*rokugatsu*	6月
July	*shichigatsu*	7月
August	*hachigatsu*	8月
September	*kugatsu*	9月
October	*jūgatsu*	10月
November	*jūichigatsu*	11月
December	*jūnigatsu*	12月

Compare these expressions with the list of "counter" numbers on p. 19. You will see that there are special terms for the first ten days of the month, the fourteeth, and the twentieth.

Yesterday was the thirty-first.
*Kinō wa **sanjū ichinichi** desu.*
昨日は31日です。

Today is the first.

*Kyō wa **tsuitachi** desu.*
今日は1日です。

Tomorrow is the second.
*Ashita wa **futsuka** desu.*
明日は2日です。

second	*futsuka*	日
third	*mikka*	3日
fourth	*yokka*	4日
fifth	*itsuka*	5日
sixth	*muika*	6日
seventh	*nanoka*	7日
eighth	*yōka*	8日
ninth	*kokonoka*	9日
tenth	*tōka*	10日

The other days of the month are designated with ordinary numbers, followed by *nichi*, or "day" (e.g., *jūninichi*, literally "twelve day," the twelfth of the month).

eleventh	*jūichinichi*	11日
twelfth	*jūninichi*	12日
thirteenth	*jūsan'nichi*	13日
fourteenth	*jūyokka*	14日
fifteenth	*jūgonichi*	15日
sixteenth	*jūrokunichi*	16日
seventeenth	*jūshichinichi*	17日
eighteenth	*jūhachinichi*	18日
nineteenth	*jūkyunichi*	19日
twentieth	*hatsuka*	20日
twenty-first	*nijū ichinichi*	21日
twenty-second	*nijū ninichi*	22日
twenty-third	*nijū san'nichi*	23日
twenty-fourth	*nijū yokka*	24日
twenty-fifth	*nijū gonichi*	25日
twenty-sixth	*nijū rokunichi*	26日
twenty-seventh	*nijū shichinichi*	27日
twenty-eighth	*nijū hachinichi*	28日
twenty-ninth	*nijū kunichi*	29日
thirtieth	*sanjū nichi*	30日
thirty-first	*sanjū ichinichi*	31日

Japanese are avid borrowers of words from other languages, particularly English, which they render into the sounds of their own language. Because these "Japanized" words sound familiar they are easy to remember, giving you a good headstart on building a useful vocabulary.

ACTIVITIES

tour	*tsuā*	ツアー
concert	*konsāto*	コンサート
honeymoon	*hanemūn*	ハネムーン
kiss	*kisu*	キス

BUSINESS

memo	*memo*	メモ
ball pen	*bōru pen*	ボールペン
message	*messēji*	メッセージ
schedule	*sukejūru*	スケジュール
calendar	*karendā*	カレンダー

BRANDS

Cartier	*Karutie*	カルティエ
Hermes	*Erumesu*	エルメス
Chanel	*Shaneru*	シャネル

BREAKFAST

toast	*tōsuto*	トースト
omelette	*omuretsu*	オムレツ
fruit	*furūtsu*	フルーツ
juice	*jūsu*	ジュース
coffee	*kōhii*	コーヒー

CITIES

Rome	*Rōma*	ローマ
Cairo	*Kairo*	カイロ
Miami	*Maiami*	マイアミ

Note that the Japanese make no attempt to duplicate the original pronunciation of a borrowed word, but merely change each syllable to the Japanese sound that best approximates it.

CLOTHES

suit	*sūtsu*	スーツ
necktie	*nekutai*	ネクタイ
jeans	*jiinzu*	ジーンズ
skirt	*sukāto*	スカート
blouse	*burausu*	ブラウス
sweater	*sētā*	セーター
handkerchief	*hankachi*	ハンカチ

COLORS

green	*guriin*	グリーン
orange	*orenji*	オレンジ
black	*burakku*	ブラック
pink	*pinku*	ピンク
red	*reddo*	レッド

COMMENTS

nonsense	*nansensu*	ナンセンス
no comment	*nō kommento*	ノーコメント

COMMUNICATIONS

telephone	*terefon*	テレフォン
fax	*fakkusu*	ファックス
radio	*rajio*	ラジオ
television	*terebi*	テレビ
video (player)	*bideo*	ビデオ

COMPUTERS

computer	*konpūtā*	コンピューター
printer	*purintā*	プリンター
data	*dēta*	データ

With the exception of *n*, Japanese sounds have no consonant endings. Thus most borrowed words will end in the Japanese vowels: *a, i, u, e,* and *o*. Note also that longer words are often shortened ("television" becomes *terebi*) and word pairs are often clipped and combined ("word processor" becomes *wāpuro*).

CONTINENTS

Africa	*Afurika*	アフリカ
Europe	*Yōroppa*	ヨーロッパ
America	*Amerika*	アメリカ

COUNTRIES

France	*Furansu*	フランス
Canada	*Kanada*	カナダ
Russia	*Roshia*	ロシア

DINNER

steak	*sutēki*	ステーキ
salad	*sarada*	サラダ
green peas	*gurin piisu*	グリンピース

DRINKS

whiskey	*uiskii*	ウイスキー
beer	*biiru*	ビール
wine	*wain*	ワイン

LUNCH

sandwich	*sandoitchi*	サンドイッチ
hamburger	*hanbāgā*	ハンバーガー
potato chips	*poteto chippusu*	ポテトチップス
cola	*kōra*	コーラ

MUSIC

piano	*piano*	ピアノ
violin	*baiorin*	バイオリン
guitar	*gitā*	ギター

With a little practice, it will become easy not only to recognize these words when Japanese use them, but to form your own Japanized terms from English.

PEOPLE

Clinton	*Kurinton*	クリントン
Picasso	*Pikaso*	ピカソ
Hemingway	*Heminguwē*	ヘミングウェイ
Stallone	*Sutarōn*	スタローン

RESTAURANT ITEMS

restaurant	*resutoran*	レストラン
knife	*naifu*	ナイフ
fork	*fōku*	フォーク
spoon	*supūn*	スプーン
menu	*menyū*	メニュー
Perrier	*Perie*	ペリエ

SPORTS

sports	*supōtsu*	スポーツ
baseball	*bēsubōru*	ベースボール
basketball	*basuketto*	バスケット
golf	*gorufu*	ゴルフ
iceskating	*aisusukēto*	アイススケート
team	*chiimu*	チーム
coach	*kōchi*	コーチ
champion	*chyanpion*	チャンピオン
home run	*hōmuran*	ホームラン
hole in one	*hōruinwan*	ホールインワン

STRUCTURES

dam	*damu*	ダム
tunnel	*tonneru*	トンネル
hotel	*hoteru*	ホテル
apartment	*apāto*	アパート
supermarket	*sūpā*	スーパー

Hints for Grammar Haters

Although it is a goal of *Fingertip Japanese* to avoid grammatical explanations, there are a few basic patterns in Japanese that allow one to substitute new vocabulary to create an unlimited number of expressions.

Examples

A principle feature of the Japanese language is that verbs come at the end of sentences, the most common verb being *desu*, meaning "is" (in the sense of "equals"). In the examples below, the particle *wa* follows and marks the subject, X, to which something, Y, is being equated:

X is Y.	*X wa Y desu.*
She's Sally.	*Kanōjo wa Sari desu.*
It's cold today.	*Kyo wa samui desu.*
Tomorrow is the tenth.	*Ashita wa tōkka desu.*

The question particle *ka* added to the verb makes the statement a question:

Is X Y?	*X wa Y desuka?*
Is she Sally?	*Kanōjo wa Sari desuka?*
Is it cold today?	*Kyo wa samui desuka?*
Is tomorrow the tenth?	*Ashita wa tōkka desuka?*

The verb *arimasu*, literally "is" or "are" (in the sense of "exists") is also quite versatile, especially when the particle *ka* is added to form a question. The negative form is *arimasen*. Notice that the particle *ga* changes to *wa* in this structure.

Is there any X?	*X ga arimasuka?*
There is X.	*X ga arimasu.*
There is no X.	*X wa arimasen.*

Do you have red wine?	*Reddo wain ga arimasuka?*
Yes, we do.	*Hai, arimasu.*
No, we don't.	*Iie, arimasen.*

Finally, the verb *kudasai* (the imperative form of the verb *kudasaru*, "to give") is very useful for making requests, with numerous examples appearing in the later chapters. Note that *onegai shimasu* ("I request that you . . ."), introduced on p. 14, may also be used for this purpose.

Give me X, please.	*X o kudasai.*
	X o onegai shimasu.
A cheeseburger, please.	*Chiizubāgā o kudasai.*
Cola, please.	*Kōra o onegai shimasu.*

You will encounter the above structures again and again in *Fingertip Japanese*, and mastering them is the key to a basic communicative ability in Japanese.

Getting Settled

A broad variety of accommodations are available in Japan, mainly due to the continued existence of traditional-style inns and hostels alongside new Western-style hotels and resorts. All of these types of establishment have associations which may be contacted for assistance (p. 195). This chapter contains all the words and phrases you will need to get settled in the hotel or inn of your choice, and to take advantage of services to make your stay more comfortable.

Types of Accommodations

hotel ホテル *hoteru*
Most Western visitors to Japan will have made reservations at a Western-style tourist hotel, comparable in price and services to hotels in other major cities around the world. English will be spoken by the staff.

business hotel ビジネス・ホテル *bijinesu hoteru*
Used by traveling Japanese business people, these are less expensive than tourist hotels and usually conveniently located near transportation centers. However, they generally offer limited amenities and the English-language proficiency of the staff may be limited.

inn 旅館 *ryokan*
These traditional accommodations will feature Japanese-style rooms (*tatami* floors, *futon* bedding, etc.), and may range in price from moderate to very expensive. Room charge usually includes dinner and

breakfast, at which Japanese food will be served. Except at *ryokan* that specialize in catering to foreign visitors, the staff will likely not speak English.

family-run guest house 民宿 *minshuku*
Literally "people's lodgings," these small and usually inexpensive accommodations, although Japanese style, lack the services generally provided by *ryokan*. Guests usually gather for meals at a common dining room, and prepare their own bedding for sleeping,

pension ペンション *penshon*
These might be considered Western-style *minshuku*, as they are generally inexpensive and family-run, but usually feature beds and Western food. Pension abound at ski and hot-spring resort areas.

youth hostel ユース・ホステル *yūsu hosteru*
Japan has both government and privately run youth hostels, which welcome students and young people.

hotsprings resort 温泉 *onsen*
Properly speaking, an *onsen* is not a type of accommodation but a hot-springs area, where you might find a variety of lodgings. Staying at a *minshuku* or *ryokan* there will allow you to experience a Japanese-style vacation in traditional surroundings.

capsule hotel カプセル・ホテル *kapuseru hoteru*
These inexpensive sleeping cubicles are found at some larger train stations, to accommodate those who have missed the last trains to distant homes. They are not recommended accommodations, but are mentioned since they have attracted media attention.

Although you'll probably arrive in Japan with a reservation, you may wish to find out about accommodations elsewhere, or take the opportunity to spend a night in traditional Japanese lodgings.

Can you recommend a good hotel in [PLACE]?
[PLACE] de ii hoteru wa arimasuka?
[場所]でいいホテルはありますか？

Can you recommend a hotel near here?
Kono chikaku ni ii hoteru wa arimasuka?
この近くにいいホテルはありますか？

the town center	*hankagai no*	繁華街の
the main sights	*kankō meisho no*	観光名所の
the train station	*eki no*	駅の
the airport	*kūko no*	空港の

Are these any Japanese-style lodgings.
Nihon shiki no yado wa arimasuka?
日本式の宿はありますか？

Can you recommend a good ryokan?
Ii ryokan wa arimasuka?
いい旅館はありますか？

an inexpensive ryokan	*yasui ryokan*	安い旅館
an inexpensive hotel	*yasui hotel*	安いホテル
a family-run guest house	*minshuku*	民宿
a business hotel	*bijinesu hoteru*	ビジネス・ホテル
a pension	*penshon*	ペンション
a youth hostel	*yūsu hosuteru*	ユースホステル
onsen lodgings	*onsen yado*	温泉宿

Please make a reservation for me.
Yoyaku o onegai shimasu.
予約をおねがいします。

ASKING ABOUT ACCOMMODATIONS 41

There is an association for each type of accommodation, and these have offices to assist you with reservations. See p. 195 for addresses and phone numbers.

How much is it per night?   (MONEY, p. 24)
Ippaku ikura desuka?
一泊いくらですか？

I'd prefer a less expensive place.
Motto yasui tokoro o onegaishimasu.
もっと安い所をおねがいします。

Have you a place under [AMOUNT] dollars?
[AMOUNT] ika no tokoro wa arimasuka?
［金額］以下の所はありますか？

What's the name of the hotel?
Hoteru no namae wa nan desuka?
ホテルの名前はなんですか？

Where is it? Can you show me on this map?
Doko desuka? Kono chiizu no doko desuka?
どこですか。この地図のどこですか？

Please write down the name and address.
Hoteru no namae to jūsho o kaite kudasai.
ホテルの名前と住所を書いてください。

How do I get there?
Dō yatte ikemasuka?
どうやって行けますか？

What's the nearest station to the hotel?
Moyori no eki wa doko desuka?
最寄りの駅はどこですか？

Reservations for main tourist hotels can be made at the airport's hotel reservation counter. For other accommodations you can get help from the Japan National Tourist Organization or the Japan Travel Bureau (p. 194).

Where's the hotel reservation counter?
Hoteru no yoyaku kauntā wa doko desuka?
ホテルの予約カウンターはどこですか？

Where's the Japan Travel Bureau office?
JTB wa doko desuka?
JTBはどこですか？

Where's the information counter?
Kankō an'naijo wa doko desuka?
観光案内所はどこですか？

I'd like to make a reservation.
Yoyaku o onegai shimasu.
予約をお願いします。

Do you have any rooms available for tonight?
Konban heya wa aitemasuka?
今晩、部屋は空いてますか？   (DAYS, p. 28)
tomorrow night *ashita no ban* 明日の晩
Sunday night *nichiyōbi no ban* 日曜日の晩

I'd like to stay one night.
Ippaku shimasu.
1泊します。
two nights *nihakku* 2泊
three nights *sanpakku* 3泊

I'd like a single room.
Shinguru no heya o onegaishimasu.
シングルの部屋をお願いします。

double room *daburu no heya* ダブルの部屋
suite *suiito* スィート

I'd like a quiet room.
Shizukana heya o onegaishimasu.
静かな部屋をお願いします。

large room   *hiroi*   広い
room with a view   *nagame no ii*   眺めのいい
no-smoking room   *kin'en no*   禁煙の

I'd like a double bed.
Daburu beddo o onegai shimasu.
ダブルベッドをお願いします。

I'd like twin beds.
Tsuin beddo o onegai shimasu.
ツインベッドをお願いします。

I'd like an extra (child's) bed.
Ekusutora (kodomo yōni) beddo o onegai shimasu.
エクストラ（子供用に）ベッドをお願いします。

How much is the room per night?   (MONEY, p. 24)
Ippaku ikura desuka?
一泊いくらですか？

Where is the hotel?
Hoteru wa doko desuka?
ホテルはどこですか？

Please write down the name and address.
Hoteru no namae to jūsho o kaite kudasai.
ホテルの名前と住所を書いて下さい。

Communications should be no problem at tourist hotels, but might at business hotels and Japanese-style accommodations. It is not a good idea to arrive at a minshuku or ryokan without a reservation, because the prospect of having to deal with the language problem may cause the innkeeper to turn you away.

Excuse me. I'm [NAME].
Sumimasen. Watashi wa [NAME] desu.
すみません。私は[名前]です。

I have a reservation.
Yoyaku shite imasu.
予約しています。

There are two of us.   (COUNTERS, p. 22)
Futari desu.
二人です。

When is check-out time?
Chekku auto wa nanji desuka?
チェック・アウトは何時ですか？

We'd like to see the room first.
Saki ni heya o misete kudasai.
先に部屋を見せてください。

Sorry, I don't have a reservation.
Sumimasen, yoyaku o shite imasen.
すみません。予約をしていません。

Do you have any rooms available?
Heya wa aite imasuka?
部屋は空いていますか？

Please help me find a room elsewhere.
Doko ka heya o sagashite kudasai.
どこか部屋を探してください。

Except for the large resort spas, Japanese inns have fewer shops and services than do Western hotels, and any special food or drink items you will require should be brought along. Note that one exception to the no-tipping policy of Japan is at top-class ryokan, where a gratuity is customarily left for room maids.

Which way is the bath?
Furo wa dokodesuka?
風呂はどこですか？。
outdoor bath *rotemburo* 露天風呂
toilet *toire* トイレ

What are the bath hours?
Furo wa nanji kara nanji made desuka?
風呂は何時から何時までですか？

What time is dinner served?
Yūshoku wa nanji desuka?
夕食は何時ですか？
breakfast *chōshoku* 朝食

Where is dinner served?
Yūshoku wa doko desuka?
夕食はどこですか？
breakfast *chōshoku* 朝食

Who is it?
Donata desuka?
どなたですか？

Just a minute . . . Come in!
Chotto matte kudasai . . . Dōzo!
ちょっと待って下さい・・・どうぞ！

Japanese Western-style hotels typically offer all the amenities of their counterparts in the West. Tipping is not the custom in Japan, and is unnecessary.

Which way is the elevator?
Erebētā wa doko desuka?
エレベーターはどこですか？

telephone	*denwa*	電話
front desk	*furonto*	フロント
concierge	*conseruje*	コンシェルジェ
bathroom	*basurūmu*	バスルーム

Is there a restaurant in the hotel?
Hoteru no naka ni restoran wa arimasuka?
ホテルのなかにレストランはありますか？

Japanese restaurant	*Washoku resutoran*	和食レストラン
Western restaurant	*Yōshoku resutoran*	洋食レストラン
coffee shop	*kōhii shoppu*	コーヒーショップ
bar	*bā*	バー
gift shop	*gifuto shoppu*	ギフトショップ
newsstand	*zasshi sutando*	雑誌スタンド
currency-exchange	*ryōgaejō*	両替所
travel counter	*ryokō annaijō*	旅行案内所
business center	*bijinesu sentā*	ビジネスセンター
sauna	*sauna*	サウナ
gym	*jimu*	ジム
swimming pool	*pūru*	プール
tennis court	*tenisu kōto*	テニスコート

Which way is it? . . . What floor is it on?
Dokodesuka? . . . Nankai desuka?
どこですか？ ・・・ 何階ですか？

When does it open? . . . When does it close?
Nanji kara desuka? . . . Nanji made desuka?
何時からですか？ ・・・ 何時までですか？

As elsewhere in Japan, many items are dispensed through vending machines. A vending area on your floor will often dispense snack foods, drinks, and basic toiletries.

This is room [NUMBER].   (NUMBERS, p. 18)
Rūmu [NUMBER] desu.
ルームナンバー［番号］です。

I'd like to have my room made up.
Heya no sōji o onegai shimasu.
部屋の掃除をお願いします。
clothes laundered *sentaku* 洗濯
clothes cleaned *dorai kuriningu*   ドライクリーニング
clothes pressed *fukuno airongake* 服のアイロンがけ

I'd like to order breakfast.
Chōshoku o onegaishimasu.
朝食をお願いします。
lunch *chūshoku* 昼食
dinner *yūshoku* 夕食

I'd like to have [ITEM]   (WESTERN FOOD, p. 128)
[ITEM] o onegaishimau.
［品物］をお願いします。

Who is it?
Donata desuka?
どなたですか？

Just a minute . . . Come in!
Chotto matte kudasai . . . Dōzo!
ちょっと待って下さい・・・どうぞ！

Keep in mind that a room in a Japanese business hotel although economical, may well be smokey and small.

The room is hot.
*Heya ga **atsui** desu.*
部屋が暑いです。
cold *samui* 寒い
smokey *tabako kusai* タバコくさい
noisy *urusai* うるさい
small *semai* 狭い

The TV doesn't work.
***Terebi** ga tsukimasen.*
テレビがつきません。
radio *rajio* ラジオ
air conditioner *eakon* エアコン
lamp *denki* 電気

I'd like to check out, please.
Chekku auto o onegaishimasu.
チェック・アウトをお願いします。

Isn't there a mistake?
Machigai ga arimasuka?
間違いがありますか？

Please give me a receipt.
Ryōshūshō o kudasai.
領収書を下さい。

Is this credit card OK?
Kurejitto kādo wa tsukaemasuka?
クレジット・カードは使えますか？

Please call a taxi for me.
Takushii o yonde kudasai.
タクシーを呼んで下さい。

In resort areas when weather permits, Japanese often don a *yukata* (a light, cotton kimono), and stroll about the grounds or streets around the inn. Watch what other guests are wearing outside and dress accordingly. Note that special outdoor slippers or *geta* (clogs) are worn with *yukata*.

Where's the closest grocery store?
Ichiban chikai sūpā wa doko desuka?
一番近いスーパーはどこですか？。
restaurant *resutoran* レストラン
liquor store *sakaya* 酒屋

Are there any interesting sights nearby?
Kono chikaku ni kankōchi wa arimasuka?
この近くに観光地はありますか？
temples *tera* 寺
shrines *jinja* 神社
art museums *bijutsukan* 美術館

Is there a bus stop nearby?
Kono chikaku ni basutei wa arimasuka?
この近くにバス停はありますか？
train station *eki* 駅
subway station *chikatetsu no eki* 地下鉄の駅
taxi stand *takushii noriba* タクシー乗り場

I'd like to go to [PLACE].
[PLACE] ni ikitai no desuga.
［場所］に行きたいのですが。

How do I get there?
Do yatte ikemasuka?
どうやって行けますか？

Do you have a name card for this hotel?
Hoteru no meishi ga arimasuka?
ホテルの名刺がありますか？

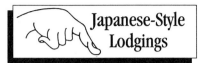

Japanese-Style Lodgings

Much has been published about the difficulty of conforming to proper etiquette and customs when staying in traditional Japanese accommodations. Most of this is overstated, as Japanese do not expect foreign visitors to act Japanese, and rules that *do* require adherence are usually fairly obvious.

• Slippers (provided) are worn inside the building, except on tatami-mat surfaces; a separate pair is worn in the toilet. You will be reminded to change footwear by the rows of slippers lined up at entryways, with street shoes placed neatly on shelves, and the pairs of plastic slippers waiting inside the toilet door.

• One custom that may not be apparent through observation is that of washing outside of the *furo* (bath); no soap or suds go in water in which the Japanese bathe. Again, should you forget you will be reminded by the washing paraphernalia (low stool, bucket, soap, and faucet or showerhead) placed away from the tub, making it obvious that there is the place to scrub. You should always lather and rinse before getting into a Japanese bath (although this rule is not followed in the *rotemburo*, or outdoor bath). In this way, the water stays clean and can be used for soaking by several people, so don't drain the tub.

• In all but the smaller *minshuku* there will be men's and women's baths, so you may wish to learn the characters for men (男) and women (女) rather than wait to see who goes in. As these characters are also used to distinguish toilets, they are quite useful.

• Many guides attempt to distinguish clearly between the services of *ryokan* (where you may be served meals in your room and your bedding is made up for you), and those of *minshuku* (where you make up and put away bedding and eat in a common room). In fact there are more or less deluxe establishments of both types and the policies may vary.

• Most guides neglect to mention two surprises you *will* likely encounter: you'll be up at the crack of dawn and on your way with no coffee! Breakfast is typically served between six and eight, and checkout time is usually ten o'clock. Breakfast, of course, is Japanese style, which means green tea rather than coffee, and typically includes rice, *miso* (soybean paste) soup, a raw egg, pickles, and perhaps fish. Although not perhaps the most enticing day-starting meal for Western palates, dinner and breakfast are included in the room charge, so this is the ideal time to sample these Japanese meals. (These days, however, some *minshuku* feature a Japanese interpretation of a Western breakfast, which may include a slice of ham, a cooked egg, and small salad.) If you cannot do without your morning coffee, bring a packet of instant; boiling water is always available in a hot pot, as it is used for tea. Dinner is not ordered, but is rather a set meal, usually with a large number of small dishes— there should be something to please every taste.

• In summary, a stay at a *ryokan* or *minshuku* provides a brief but surprisingly comprehensive introduction to the everyday customs, etiquette, and foods of traditional Japan, and really should not be missed.

Getting Around

A small country with a large population, Japan has developed a dense transportation infrastructure capable of efficiently moving great numbers of people over relatively short distances. All four of Japan's main islands are now connected by bridges or tunnels, some of which rank among the most impressive civil engineering projects in the world. This chapter contains the words and phrases you will need to travel in Japan, whether by plane or train for intercity travel, or by subway, bus, or rental car for local travel.

Types of Transportation

taxi タクシー *takushii*
Taxis are new and clean and their drivers courteous and honest, although you may encounter cabbies who choose to avoid potential language problems by passing you by. Taxis are relatively expensive, however, and drivers generally do not speak English.

subway 地下鉄 *chikatetsu*
Subways are clean, safe, fast, and run on time. Drawbacks are the lack of late-night service (lines begin closing after 11:30), and crowds at peak hours (including the last trains). Although subways systems like that of Tokyo may appear dauntingly complex, lines are color-coded and English-language maps are available.

bus バス *basu*
Many Japanese buses are oddly old-fashioned, often with plush seats and wooden floors. Although riding

above ground is grand for sightseeing, dense city traffic makes buses unsuitable if you are pressed for time.

train 電車 *densha*
Rail service in Japan is perhaps the best in the world. The six companies that make up Japan Railways operate more than 25,000 trains daily over more than 13,000 miles of track, including the high-speed Shinkansen systems (the "Bullet Train"), traveling at speeds up to 120 miles an hour. Although the Japanese rail system is extensive and complex, the efficiency of its operations and the courtesy of its staff makes it relatively easy to use. Japanese trains are punctual, so to allow yourself plenty of time to find the right platform and get aboard. A good rule of thumb is the bigger the station the earlier you should arrive.

airplane 飛行機 *hikōki*
Japan's 79 major airports are served by the domestic operations of the nation's international carriers—JAL (Japan Air Lines), ANA (All Nippon Airways), and JAS (Japan Air System), as well as local carriers. Most international visitors arrive in Japan at Narita (officially known as the New Tokyo International Airport), about 80 kilometers east of the capital. Domestic flights from Tokyo depart from both Narita and from Haneda Airport, to the south of the city.

rental car レンタカー *rentakā*
It is best to hold an International Driver's License and call ahead to reserve if you require a car immediately after getting off a train or plane. Although Japanese roads are often congested, rental cars are convenient for touring away from major urban areas—take the train and pick up a rental car at your destination.

As a taxi from Narita into the city may run $200, most visitors choose to take a train or "airport limousine" (actually a bus). Which to choose depends upon the location of your hotel or which part of the city you wish to visit first. The limousine bus stops at major tourist hotels, as well as the Tokyo City Air Terminal (known as "Tee-Cat," from its acronym TCAT) at Hakozaki, at the center of the city.

Which way is the Keisei Line?
Keisei sen wa doko desuka?
京成線はどこですか？

JR Line	*JR sen*	JR線
airport limousine	*kūkō basu*	空港バス
taxi stand	*takushii noriba*	タクシーのりば

I'd like to go to Keisei Ueno Station.
Keisei Ueno Eki ni ikitai no desuga.
京成上野駅に行きたいのですが。

Tokyo Station	*Tōkyō Eki*
	東京駅
Shinjuku Station	*Shinjuku Eki*
	新宿駅
Hakozaki Terminal	*Hakozaki Tāminaru*
	箱崎ターミナル
Haneda Airport	*Haneda Kūkō*
	羽田空港
Tokyo Hilton Hotel	*Tōkyō Hiruton Hoteru*
	東京ヒルトンホテル
New Otani Hotel	*Hoteru Nyū Ōtani*
	ホテルニューオータニ
Imperial Hotel	*Teikoku Hoteru*
	帝国ホテル
Hotel Okura	*Hoteru Ōkura*
	ホテルオークラ

The Keisei Line will take you to Ueno, in northeast Tokyo, while JR trains will take you either to Tokyo Station, in the center of the city, or Shinjuku Station, to the west. Both lines run non-stop express trains between the airport and Tokyo. The Keisei is called the "Skyliner"; the JR's is called the "Narita Express."

I'd like to take the Skyliner.
Sukairainā ni noritai no desuga.
スカイライナーに乗りたいのですが。

I'd like to take the Narita Express.
Narita Ekusupuresu ni noritai no desuga.
成田エクスプレスに乗りたいのですが。

Smoking car, please.
Kitsuen sha o onegaishimasu.
喫煙車をお願いします。

Non-smoking, please.
Kin'en sha o onegaishimasu.
禁煙車をお願いします。

Two tickets, please.   (COUNTERS, p. 23)
Nimai kudasai.
二枚ください。

How much is the fare?   (MONEY, p. 24)
Ikura desuka?
いくらですか？

Which platform does the train leave from?
Nanban sen desuka?
何番線ですか？

Which way is the platform?
Noriba wa doko desuka?
乗り場はどこですか？

TAXIS

Taxis can be hailed on the streets, at taxi stands, or in front of main hotels. A red light, rather than green, indicates a free cab. Japanese taxi doors are operated by the drivers; wait for the doors to be opened for you. See p. 69 for information about using landmarks to reach your destination.

I'd like to go to this address.
Kono jūsho ni itte kudasai.
この住所に行ってください。

I'd like to go to [DESTINATION].
[DESTINATION] made itte kudasai.
[住所]まで行ってください。

It's near [LANDMARK].
[LANDMARK] no chikaku desu.
[場所]の近くです。

How long will it take?
Nanpun gurai desuka?
何分ぐらいですか？

Take me to the nearest train station.
Moyori no eki e itte kudasai.
最寄りの駅へ行ってください。

Turn left at the next intersection.
Tsugi no kōsaten o hidari desu.
次の交差点を左です。

Turn right at the next intersection.
Tsugi no kōsaten o migi desu.
次の交差点を右です。

Go straight ahead.
Massugu itte kudasai.
まっすぐ行ってください。

A receipt will be provided upon request, and no tipping is required. (An exception is a hired car for a specific period, whose driver may be tipped to show appreciation for courteous service.) It is always best to carry the address of your destination, written in Japanese.

Please stop after the intersection.
Kōsaten no mukō de tomatte kudasai.
交差点のむこうで止まってください。

Please stop before the intersection.
Kōsaten no temae de tomatte kudasai.
交差点の手前で止まってください。

It's a little further.
Mō sukoshi saki desu.
もう少し先です。

I think we passed it. Please turn around.
Ikisugita yō desu. Modotte kudasai.
行き過ぎたようです。戻ってください。

Please let me off here.
Koko de orimasu.
ここで降ります。

Please wait a moment.
Chotto matte kudasai.
ちょっと待ってください。

Please wait for me here.
Koko de matte ite kudasai.
ここで待っていてください。

May I have a receipt?
Reshiito o kudasai.
レシートをください。

Maps in subway stations show fares to various destinations. If you cannot figure out your fare, buy the least expensive ticket and show it at the gate when you get off; the ticket collector there will tell you how much you owe (or take it from your outstretched palm full of coins). Most station names will appear on at least some signs in romanized Japanese, under the Japanese characters.

Excuse me, where's the closest subway station?
Sumimasen, moyori no eki wa doko desuka?
すみません。最寄りの駅はどこですか？

Which line goes to [DESTINATION]?
[DESTINATION] e wa dono chikatetsu ga ikimasuka?
［場所］へは、どの地下鉄が行きますか？

Which way to the Ginza Line?
Ginza sen wa doko desuka?
銀座線はどこですか？

Marunouchi	丸ノ内
Hibiya	日比谷
Chiyoda	千代田
Hanzōmon	半蔵門

Where can I buy a ticket?
Kippu uriba wa doko desuka?
キップ売り場はどこですか？

Which machine do I use?
Dono jidōhanbaiki desuka?
どの自動販売機ですか？。

How much is the fare?
Ikura desuka?
いくらですか？。

New subway cars are quite high-tech, with illuminated signs showing upcoming stations, in both English and Japanese, and lights indicating which side of the train to get off. On older subway cars, you'll have to keep track of your progress by means of the maps over the doors, or ask fellow passengers to help you out.

Excuse me, is this seat taken?
Sumimasen, aite imasuka?
すみません、空いていますか？

What station is this?
Koko wa dono eki desuka?
ここはどこの駅ですか？

What station is next?
Tsugi wa doko desuka?
次はどこですか？

Does this train go to [DESTINATION]?
[DESTINATION] ni ikimasuka?
［場所］に行きますか？

Do I have to change trains?
Norikaemasuka?
乗り変えますか？

Could you tell me when we get to [DESTINATION]?
[DESTINATION] ni tsuitara oshiete kudasai.
［場所］に着いたら教えてください。

How many stations is it?
Sore wa ikutsume no eki desuka?
それはいくつ目の駅ですか？

Buying a reserved round-trip ticket will eliminate anxiety about return seating, especially on weekend day trips to popular tourist destinations such as Nikko. Be sure to check for express or limited express (even faster) service to your destination.

I want to go to [DESTINATION].
[DESTINATION] ni ikitai no desuga.
［場所］に行きたいのですが。

I'd like to leave as soon as possible.   (TIME, pp. 25-27)
Sugu noritai no desuga.
すぐ乗りたいのですが。

this evening	*konban*	今晩
around 1:00 p.m.	*gogo ichiji goro*	午後一時頃

I'd like to return tomorrow.   (DAYS, DATES, pp. 28-30)
Asu modorimasu.
明日もどります。

Monday evening	*getsuyō(bi) no yoru*	月曜(日)の夜
on the twenty-first	*nijōichinichi ni*	21日に

I'd like a one-way ticket.
Katamichi kippu o kudasai.
片道切符をください。

round-trip ticket	*ōfuku*	往復
reserved seat	*shitei seki*	指定席
no-smoking car seat	*kin'en seki*	禁煙席
smoking car seat	*kitsuen seki*	喫煙席
express ticket	*tokkyū ken*	特急
limited express ticket	*kyūko ken*	急行

How much is the fare?
(Jōshaken wa) ikura desuka?
（乗車券は）いくらですか？

I'd like one ticket.   (COUNTERS, p. 23)
Ichimai kudasai.
1枚ください。

| two tickets | *nimai* | 2枚 |
| three tickets | *sanmai* | 3枚 |

What time does the train leave?
Nanji ni demasuka?
何時に出ますか？

Which platform does it leave from?
Nanbansen kara demasuka?
何番線から出ますか？

Which way is the platform?
Hōmu wa doko desuka?
ホームはどこですか？

How long does it take to get there?
Soko made jikan wa dono kurai desuka?
そこまで時間はどのくらいですか？

Do I have to change trains?
Norikaemasuka?
乗り換えますか？

Where do I change trains?
Doko de norikaemasuka?
どこで乗り換えますか？

The Shinkansen, or "Bullet Train," allows only a few minutes for boarding. If you have a Green Car (deluxe) or reserved-seat ticket, you need only get aboard the right train and find your set eventually. However, if you have no reservation and wish to sit, you should be waiting in a line that will lead to a door in a carriage with "free seating."

Excuse me, is this the right platform for [PLACE]?
Sumimasen, [PLACE] yuki wa, kono hōmu desuka?
すみません、[場所]行きは、このホームですか？

Is this the platform for [TRAIN NAME OR NUMBER].
[TRAIN NAME OR NUMBER] wa, kono hōmu desuka?
[電車名／番号]は、このホームですか？

Where do I stand for free seating?
Jiyūseki wa, dono hen desuka?
自由席は、どの辺ですか？

Where do I stand for the Green Car?
Guriin sha wa, dono hen desuka?
グリーン車は、どの辺ですか？

How many more stops until [PLACE]?
[PLACE] made, ato ikutsu desuka?
[場所]まで、あといくつですか？

Would you tell when we stop at [PLACE]?
[PLACE] ni tsuitara oshiete kudasai.
[場所]に着いたら教えて下さい。

Which way is the dining car?
***Shokudōsha** wa doko desuka?*
食堂車はどこですか？

telephone	*denwa*	電話
restroom	*toire*	トイレ

On city buses, fares are usually fixed; the amount is posted outside near the door or on the coin-deposit box, and is paid when boarding. On longer-distance rural buses, each passenger takes a numbered ticket when boarding; the number corresponds to a fare, indicated on frequently updated display over the driver's head, and is paid when getting off. For long-distance buses originating at terminals, tickets are purchased in advance.

Does this bus go to [PLACE]?
Kono basu wa [PLACE] ni ikimasuka?
このバスは[場所]に行きますか？

What's the best place to get off?
Doko de orireba yoi desuka?
どこで降りれば良いですか？

Is this where I get off for [PLACE]?
[PLACE] wa koko de oriru no desuka?
[場所]はここで降りるのですか？

How much is the fare?
Ikura desuka?
いくらですか？

Where do I put the money?
Okane wa doko ni iremasuka?
お金はどこに入れますか？

Where do I buy a ticket?
Kippu wa doko de kaemasuka?
キップはどこで買えますか？

Is this [PLACE]?
Koko wa [PLACE] desuka?
ここは[場所]ですか？

Domestic airfares are regulated by the government, so there is little benefit from comparison shopping, except for package deals (see p. 68).

I want to fly to [PLACE].
[PLACE] made tobitai no desuga.
［場所］まで飛びたいのですが。

What times are there flights?
Sono furaito no sukejūru o oshiette kudasai.
そのフライトのスケジュールを教えて下さい。

What time does the plane arrive at [PLACE]?
[PLACE] ni wa nanji ni tsukimasuka?
［場所］には何時に着きますか？

I'd like to leave this evening.   (TIME, pp. 25–27)
Kyō no yūgata ni shuppatsu shitai no desuga.
今日の夕方に出発したいのですが。

| tomorrow morning | *asu no asa* | 明日の朝 |
| around 1:00 p.m. | *gogo ichiji gurai* | 午後1時ぐらい |

I'd like to return tomorrow. (DAYS, DATES, pp. 28–31)
Ashita ni modotte kitai no desuga.
明日に戻って来たいのですが。

| Tuesday evening | *kāyobi no ban* | 火曜の晩 |
| on the fifteenth | *jūgonichi* | 15日 |

I'd like a one-way ticket.
Katamichi kippu o kudasai.
片道の旅券を下さい。

round-trip	*ōfuku*	往復
economy-class	*ekonomii kurasu*	エコノミークラス
first-class ticket	*fāsto kurasu*	ファーストクラス

In general, one-way fares are half of round-trip fares. There may be discounts on round-trip travel completed within seven days, and there are discounts for young people, women's groups, and senior citizens.

How much is the fare?
Ikura desuka?
いくらですか？

I'd like one ticket.   (COUNTERS, p. 23)
Ichimai kudasai.
1枚下さい。

I'd like to check this bag.
Kono baggu o chekku shimasu.
このバッグをチェックします。

I'd like to check these.
Kore o chekku shimasu.
これをチェックします。

Can I carry this bag on the plane?
Kono baggu wa mochi komemasuka?
このバッグは持ち込めますか？

Which gate does it leave from?
Tōjō guchi wa nanban gēto desuka?
塔乗口は何番ゲートですか？

Which way is the gate?
Gēto wa doko desuka?
ゲートはどこですか？

Is there meal service?
Shokuji no sābisu wa arimasuka?
食事のサービスはありますか？

Traveling around Japan by rented car is not a great transportation bargain, due to the high cost of gasoline (about $4.00 per gallon) and tolls; likewise urban congestion prevents automobiles from being convenient for sightseeing in the cities. Still, driving is a great way to see the countryside. Reserve a car at a train station close to the area you wish to explore. You can pick it up and drop it off there, taking the train to avoid congested roads to and from the city.

I'd like to reserve a car.
Yoyaku o onegaishimasu.
予約をお願いします。

I'd like to use it for one day. (DAYS, DATES, pp. 28–31)
Ichinichi karitai no desuga.
1日借りたいのですが。

two days   *futsuka*   2日
one week   *isshūkan*   1週間

I'd like a car large enough for three people.
San'nin ga noreru kuruma o onegaishimasu.
3人が乗れる車をお願いします。

four   *yonin*   4人
six   *rokunin*   6人

I'd like the most economical model available.
Ichiban yasui kuruma o onegaishimasu.
一番安い車をお願いします。

I'd like the roomiest model available.
Ichiban ōkii kuruma o onegaishimasu.
一番大きい車をお願いします。

Although visitors may legally drive in Japan with valid home-country licenses, rental car agencies are more comfortable when presented with an International Driver's License, which must be obtained before arriving. In the U.S., International Driver's Licenses are available at local offices of the American Automobile Association, upon presentation of valid license and a small fee.

I'd like automatic transmission.
Otomatikku sha o onegaishimasu.
オートマチック車をお願いします。

I'd like manual transmission.
Manyuaru sha o onegaishimasu.
マニュアル車をお願いします。

How much is the rental?
Ikura desuka?
いくらですか？

Is insurance included?
Hoken wa haitte imasuka?
保険は入っていますか？

Is there an emergency phone number?
Kinkyū no renraku saki wa nanban desuka?
緊急の連絡先は何番ですか？

Do you have a road map?
Rōdo mappu wa arimasuka?
ロードマップはありますか？

Planes, Trains, and Automobiles

Observers of their penchant for group travel often assume that Japanese are afraid to travel abroad alone. The truth is simply that they are more comfortable with well-planned activities, and thus are equally fond of domestic package tours. These can be real bargains for the budget-minded foreign visitor: ski packages to Hokkaido, for example, will often include hotels and meals for less than the cost of ordinary round-trip air-fare. You are free to go sightseeing, of course, rather than ski.

• If you are planning extended rail travel during a limited stay in Japan, a Japan Railpass is a must. Available for periods of one, two, or three weeks, a rail-pass allows unlimited miles aboard both regular and high-speed (Shinkansen) trains, at ordinary or "Green Car" (deluxe) levels of service. They must be purchased outside of Japan (see p. 196 for contact numbers). To make maximum use of your railpass, it is a good idea to consult with Japan Rail (JR) or Japan Travel Bureau (JTB) personnel upon your arrival in Japan. If you have not purchased a railpass, you may still be able to take advantage of special passes (unlimited travel during a specified time period, especially in summer), and discounts for groups of four or more. Japan Rail also operates hotels, and offers many economical packages combining train fare and lodging.

• The urban rail system in Japanese cities often appears confusing because here public and private inter-city rail systems mix with metropolitan or private subway lines. A subway train may run on elevated tracks into a station where you must descend underground to catch a train. However, the same boarding procedure applies to all: you must buy a ticket to get through the gate (whether manned or automated) to get on the train, and you must turn in your ticket to exit a gate. You must have a ticket to ride.

• To reach your destination successfully the first time by taxi, the importance of having a reliable address (that is, written in Japanese by a Japanese) cannot be overstated. The same driver who will throw up his hands at your verbal directions will cruise endlessly on your behalf in search of a destination he is convinced truly exists, as evidenced by real Japanese script. When heading by taxi to a destination you are familiar with, or one to which you go to regularly, rather than provide a verbal address it is easier to give the name of a recognized "landmark." This might be a train or subway station in the area, a major intersection, hotel, building, or tourist attraction.

• Finally, if you are brave enough to seek out an address on foot, you will soon discover that most Japanese cities and towns are not laid out in a grid pattern, but divided into irregular and successively smaller named or numbered units. Moreover, house and building numbers are not necessarily consecutive, but relate to how long ago the property was established. If you cannot read Japanese street maps (which are posted conveniently and conspicuously), you should have a Japanese address in hand to show to the policeman at the *kōban*, the local police box.

Getting Acquainted

Fingertip Japanese is designed as phrase book rather than a language book, so it will not help you through a dialogue on, say, differing aesthetic values of East and West. However, Japanese seem to enjoy lively exchanges about fairly trivial topics, and you may be surprised at how much you can both contribute and learn with some basic words and phrases. This chapter contains expressions to help you get a conversation started or keep one going.

Ten Things You Can Always Say to Japanese

Busy?
忙しいですか？
Isogashii desuka?
A Japanese who is not too busy may be suspected of being unsuccessful and unhappy, so the typically cheerful response to this question, often used as a greeting, is *Tai hen isogashii!* ("Incredibly busy!").

Hot, isn't it?
暑いですね？
Atsui desu ne?
Like people everywhere, Japanese love to gripe about the weather, so a comment about the temperature also serves as a friendly greeting, often replacing *Konnichiwa* ("Hello"). If it is very cold *Samui desu ne?* is the appropriate expression.

How are you doing?

元気ですか？

Genki desuka?

Like its English equivalent, this expression (literally "Healthy?"), can elicit either a perfunctory response or an actual answer cataloguing the good or ill that has recently befallen one. The typical set response is *Hai, okagesamade,* something like "Yes, thanks to you."

Excuse me, where is the train station?

すみません、駅はどこですか？

Sumimasen, eki wa doko desuka?

Without suggesting that you deliberately act lost for the purpose of striking up a conversation, let it again be noted that most Japanese are ever ready to come to the aid of foreign visitors in distress, and thus many acquaintances have actually been made this way. In this useful structure, *eki*, or "station," can be replaced by whatever you may be seeking.

How old is he (or she) ?

何歳ですか？

Nansai desuka?

As in English, this question can be politely asked only about babies and children; likewise, as in the West, it is usually politely and proudly answered. Perhaps because Japanese families are small (averaging 1.5 children), offspring are doted upon, and often allowed a freedom of action and expression that leaves visitors pondering how they manage to grow into such well-mannered adults. A nice follow-up remark to the above would *Kawaii ne?*, meaning "Cute, isn't she (or he)?"

What's this?

これは何ですか？

Kore wa nan desuka?

This wonderfully all-purpose question can be used to inquire about anything from crafts and tools to food-stuffs and clothing. It may inspire any reaction from an explanation in broken English to a demonstration or pantomime.

Delicious, isn't it?

おいしいですね？

Oishii desune?

If the previous expression is used to inquire about food, it will likely be followed by a trial tasting, after which this comment may be appropriate. If you're afraid that such a favorable remark may result in your having to ingest more of something you cannot bear, saying *Kekko desu* ("That's fine," with the sense of "Enough, thanks") will get you off the hook politely.

How do you say it in Japanese?

日本語で何といいますか？

Nihongo de nan to iimasuka?

This expression is an essential tool for those who wish to expand their Japanese vocabularies, but it is useful even for those who do not; for example, it can be used to find out the name of a delicious dish you have discovered so that you can get it again elsewhere.

Sorry, I can only speak a little Japanese.
すみません、日本語は少しだけ出来ます。
Sumimasen, Nihongo wa sukoshi dake dekimasu.
It is possible that your speaking Japanese might lead others to believe that you comprehend much more than you actually do. This expression will help slow things down if you get in over your head in a Japanese conversation.

Sorry, I don't speak Japanese.
すみません、日本語はぜんぜん出来ません。
Sumimasen, Nihongo wa zen zen dekimasen.
This expression, especially when accompanied by waving a hand in front of your (smiling) face, will put a fair damper on any conversation in Japanese, and thus should only be used if you actually wish to extricate yourself from any discussion.

Some of the following words and sentences were presented in the first chapter (pp. 14–17) and are explained in detail there.

Good morning.
Ohayō gozaimasu.
おはようございます。

Good day.
Konnichiwa.
こんにちは。

Good evening.
Konbanwa.
こんばんは。

How are you?
Genki desuka?
元気ですか？

Fine, thanks.
Hai, okagesamade.
はい、おかげさまで。

How do you do?
Hajimemashite.
はじめまして。

How do you do?
Doozo yoroshiku.
どうぞよろしく。

Hot, isn't it?
Atsui, desune?
暑いですね。

Beautiful day, isn't it?
Ii tenki desune?
いい天気ですね？

Conversational starters need not be restricted to greetings. Questions eliciting information, regardless of how useful, are often a better bet for establishing a dialogue.

What's this?
Kore wa nan desuka?
これは何ですか？

What's it for?
Kore o dō suru no desuka?
これをどうするのですか？

How is it used?
Kore wa dō tsukau no desuka?.
これはどう使うのですか？

Do you eat this?
Kore wa taberaremasuka?
これは食べられますか？

Do you know what it's called in English?
Sore wa Eigo de nanto iimasuka?
それは英語で何といいますか？

How do you say that in Japanese?
Nihongo de nanto iimasuka?
日本語で何といいますか？

Can you tell me how to get here?   (showing address)
Koko ni dō yatte ikunoka oshiete kuremasuka?
ここにどうやって行くのか教えてくれますか？

Can you tell me how to use this?   (telephone, etc.)
Kore o dō yatte tsukauka oshiete kuremasuka?
これをどうやって使うか教えてくれますか？

New Japanese acquaintances will naturally be curious about who you are, where you are from, your work, interests, and family. See p. 95 for information on how to say your name in Japanese.

I'm Anne.
An desu.
アンです。

Tom	*Tomu*	トム
Sarah	*Sara*	サラ
Lenny	*Renii*	レニー

I'm American.
Amerika jin desu.
アメリカ人です。

Australian	*Ōsutoraria jin*	オーストラリア人
English	*Igirisu jin*	イギリス人
Canadian	*Kanada jin*	カナダ人

I'm from New York.
Nyūyōku kara kimashita.
ニューヨークから来ました。

Montreal	*Montoriōru*	モントリオール
London	*Rondon*	ロンドン
Sydney	*Shidonii*	シドニー

I'm a teacher.
Sensei desu.
先生です。

student	*gakusei*	学生
businessman	*bijinesuman*	ビジネスマン
doctor	*isha*	医者
engineer	*enjinia*	エンジニア
journalist	*jānarisuto*	ジャーナリスト
lawyer	*bengoshi*	弁護士
salesman	*sērusu man*	セールスマン

These patterns and substitutions can be used to state your interests in various activities and subjects or, if you are a student, your major.

I'm interested in history.
Rekishi ni kyōmi ga arimasu.
歴史に興味があります。

I'm studying architecture.
Kenchiku o benkyō shite imasu.
建築を勉強しています。

archaeology	*kōkogaku*	考古学
art	*bijutsu*	美術
computers	*konpyūtā*	コンピューター
design	*dezain*	デザイン
economics	*keizai*	経済
history	*rekishi*	歴史
literature	*bungaku*	文学
mathematics	*sūgaku*	数学
music	*ongaku*	音楽
philosophy	*tetsugaku*	哲学
physics	*butsurigaku*	物理学
science	*kagaku*	科学

I enjoy reading.
Dokusho ga suki desu.
読書が好きです。

music	*ongaku*	音楽
gardening	*niwa shigoto*	庭仕事
sports	*supōtsu*	スポーツ
movies	*eiga*	映画
theater	*engeki*	演劇
photography	*shashin*	写真
travel	*ryokō*	旅行
cooking	*ryōri*	料理

The following can be used to express more precisely
your taste in music, movies, books, and film.

I like listening to classical music.
Kurashikku o kikuno ga suki desu.
クラシックを聞くのが好きです。

rock 'n' roll	*rokkun rōru*	ロックンロール
country	*kantorii*	カントリー
jazz	*jyazu*	ジャズ

I play the violin.
Baiorin o hikimasu.
バイオリンを弾きます。

guitar	*gitā*	ギター
piano	*piano*	ピアノ
saxophone	*sakkusu*	サックス
trumpet	*toranpetto*	トランペット
clarinet	*kurarinetto*	クラリネット

I like to read fiction.
Fikushon ga suki desu.
フィクションが好きです。

non-fiction	*non fikushon*	ノンフィクション
poetry	*shi*	詩
mysteries	*misuterii*	ミステリー
science fiction	*saiensu fikushon*	サイエンス・フィクション
short stories	*tanpen shosetsu*	短編小説

I like historical movies.
Rekishi eiga ga suki desu.
歴史映画が好きです。

science fiction	*saiensu fikushon*	サイエンス・フィクション
documentaries	*dokyumentarii*	ドキュメンタリー
comedies	*komedii*	コメディー
musicals	*myūzikaru*	ミュージカル
thrillers	*surirā*	スリラー

The responses on pp. 76–83 are elicited by the basic questions ("Do you like baseball?") that Japanese learn in their English classes. Japanese are often thrilled to be able to try them out on real, live visitors from abroad. They will also be pleased, naturally, if you express an interest in Japanese culture.

I like baseball.
Yakyū ga suki desu.
野球が好きです。

football	*futto bōru*	フットボール
softball*s*	*sofuto bōru*	ソフトボール
basketball	*basuketto bōru*	バスケットボール
bicycling	*saikuringu*	サイクリング
golf	*gorufu*	ゴルフ
rugby	*ragubii*	ラグビー
soccer	*sakkā*	サッカー
swimming	*suiei*	水泳
tennis	*tenisu*	テニス

I'm interested in Japanese architecture.
*Nihon no **kenchiku** ni kyomi ga arimasu.*
日本の建築に興味があります。

business	*bijinesu*	ビジネス
cinema	*eiga*	映画
crafts	*kōgei*	工芸
culture	*bunka*	文化
dance	*buyō*	舞踊
flower arrangement	*ikebana*	生花
food	*tabemono*	食べ物
history	*rekishi*	歴史
literature	*bungaku*	文学
martial arts	*bujutsu*	武術
music	*ongaku*	音楽
theater	*engeki*	演劇

Japanese will also be curious about your family and your marital status. Although inquiries about the latter may seem prying, Japanese seem less constrained by ordinary proprieties when conversing in English with non-Japanese visitors, who have a reputation for being frank.

Yes, I'm married.
Hai, kekkon shite imasu.
はい、結婚しています。

No, I'm single.
Iie, dokushin desu.
いいえ、独身です。

We have three children.   (COUNTERS, p. 22)
Kodomo ga sannin imasu.
子供が3人います。

I have one younger brother.
Otōto ga hitori imasu.
弟が1人います。

two younger sisters	*imōto ga futari*	妹が2人
three older brothers	*ani ga sannin*	兄が3人
four older sisters	*ane ga yonin*	姉が4人

I'm the oldest son (daughter).
Watashi wa chōnan (chōjo) desu.
私は長男（長女）です。

I'm the youngest.
Suekko desu.
末っ子です。

I'm an only child.
Hitorikko desu.
1人っ子です。

Japanese will likewise be curious about what you are doing in their country, especially the purpose of your trip and the details of your itinerary.

I'm in Japan on business.
Shigoto de kimashita.
仕事で来ました。

| on vacation | *bakeshon* | バケーション |
| to study Japanese | *nihongo no benkyō* | 日本語の勉強 |

I'll be here for a few days.
Ni, san nichi iru tsumori desu.
2、3日いるつもりです。

| a week | *isshūkan* | 1週間 |
| two weeks | *nishūkan* | 2週間 |

I came three days ago.
Mikka mae ni kimashita
3日前に来ました。

| two weeks | *nishūkan* | 2週間 |
| one month | *ikkagetsu kan* | 一ヵ月間 |

Yesterday I went to [PLACE].
Kinō [PLACE] e ikimashita.
昨日[地名]へ行きました。

I'm on my way to [PLACE].
[PLACE] e iku tochū desu.
[地名]へ行く途中です。

I plan to go to [PLACE].
[PLACE] e iku yotei desu.
[地名]へ行く予定です。

Most of all, Japanese seem insatiably curious about what non-Japanese think of them and their country. This information is usually sought by using the far too general question (in English or Japanese), "How do you like Japan?"

I find (Japan) quite interesting.
Totemo omoshiroi to omoimasu.
とてもおもしろいと思います。

　　the counryside beautiful
　　inaka wa totemo utsukushii
　　田舎はとても美しい
　　as beautiful as I had expected
　　omotte itayōni kirei
　　思っていたようにきれい

I find Japanese very kind.
*Nihonjin wa **totemo shinsetsu** dato omoimasu.*
日本人はとても親切だと思います。

somewhat aloof	*dokoka tsumetai*	どこか冷たい
friendly	*atatakai*	暖かい
unfriendly	*tsumetai*	冷たい
very polite	*totemo regi tadashii*	とても礼儀正しい
too polite	*teinei sugiru*	ていねい過ぎる

I don't know, I just arrived.
Mada tsuita bakari de yoku wakarimasen.
まだ着いたばかりでよくわかりません。

I'm having a great time.
Totemo tanoshinde imasu.
とても楽しんでいます。

I'm not having such a good time.
Amari tanoshiku arimasen.
あまり楽しくありません。

Your replies to direct questions about your views on Japan may depend less on your actual opinion than your decision about how candid and precise you wish to be in a casual conversation.

I love Japanese food.
Nihonshoku ga sukidesu.
日本食が好きです。

I don't really care for Japanese food.
Nihonshoku ga amari suki dewa arimasen.
日本食があまり好きではありません。

Japanese eat a lot of Western-style food.
Nihonjin ga yōshoku o yoku tabemasu.
日本人が洋食をよく食べます。

Japanese restaurants are noisy.
Resutoran ga urusai.
レストランがうるさい。

Japanese cities have too few parks.
Machi ni kōen ga sukunai.
町に公園が少ない。

I love Japan — the food, people, culture, everything.
Watashi wa nihon ga suki desu — Nihonshoku, hitobito, bunka, Nihon no subete ga suki desu.
私は日本が好きです―日本食、人々、文化、日本の全てが好きです。

Japan seems just like Iowa.
Nihon wa Amerika no Aiowashū to sokkuri desu.
日本はアメリカのアイオワ州とそっくりです。

That's a joke.
Sore wa jōdan desu.
それは冗談です。

ADJECTIVES

To express your opinion it is useful to know some adjectives. This is not as easy to do in Japanese as in some other languages, for Japanese adjectives, like Japanese verbs, change with tense. Read across the page for present and past, positive and negative forms.

ADJECTIVE	It is …	It was …
cold	*samui desu* 寒いです	*samukatta desu* 寒かったです
hot	*atsui desu* 暑いです	*atsukatta desu* 暑かったです
convenient	*benri desu* 便利です	*benri deshita* 便利でした
good	*ii desu* いいです	*yokatta desu* よかったです
bad	*warui desu* 悪いです	*warukatta desu* 悪かったです
pretty	*kirei desu* きれいです	*kirei deshita* きれいでした
far	*tōi* 遠いです	*tōkatta desu* 遠かったです
near	*chikai desu* 近いです	*chikakatta desu* 近かったです
expensive	*takai desu* 高いです	*takakatta desu* 高かったです
cheap	*yasui desu* 安いです	*yasukatta desu* 安かったです
big	*okii desu* 大きいです	*okikatta desu* 大きかったです
small	*chiisai desu* 小さいです	*chiisakatta desu* 小さかったです
long	*nagai desu* 長いです	*nagakatta desu* 長かったです
short	*mijikai desu* 短いです	*mijikakatta desu* 短かったです
light	*karui desu* 軽いです	*karukatta desu* 軽かったです
heavy	*omoi desu* 重いです	*omokatta desu* 重かったです
enough	*jūbu na desu* 十分です	*jūbu deshita* 十分でした

When the subject is understood, these expressions can stand alone. If a subject is required, it should be followed by the particle *wa* to make a complete sentence (see p. 36). For example: *Kino wa samuku arimasen deshita*, "Yesterday wasn't cold."

It isn't …	It wasn't …
samuku arimasen	*samuku arimasen deshita*
寒くありません	寒くありませんでした
atsuku arimasen	*atsuku arimasen deshita*
暑くありません	暑くありませんでした
benri dewa arimasen	*benri ja arimasen deshita*
便利ではありません	便利じゃありませんでした
yoku arimasen	*yoku arimasen deshita*
良くありません	良くありませんでした
waruku arimasen	*waruku arimasen deshita*
悪くありません	悪くありませんでした
kirei ja arimasen	*kirei ja arimasen deshita*
きれいじゃありません	きれいじゃありませんでした
tōku arimasen	*tōku arimasen deshita*
遠くありません	遠くありませんでした
chikaku arimasen	*chikaku arimasen deshita*
近くありません	近くありませんでした
takaku arimasen	*takaku arimasen deshita*
高くありません	高くありませんでした
yasuku arimasen	*yasuku arimasen deshita*
安くありません	安くありませんでした
okiku arimasen	*okiku arimasen deshita*
大きくありません	大きくありませんでした
chiisaku arimasen	*chiisaku arimasen deshita*
小さくありません	小くありませんでした
nagaku arimasen	*nagaku arimasen deshita*
長くありません	長くありませんでした
mijikaku arimasen	*mijikaku arimasen deshita*
短くありません	短かくありませんでした
karuku arimasen	*karuku arimasen deshita*
軽くありません	軽くありませんでした
omoku arimasen	*omoku arimasen deshita*
重くありません	重くありませんでした
jūbu ja arimasen	*jūbu ja arimasen deshita*
十分じゃありません	十分じゃありませんでした

Turnabout is fair play, and the best way to get a break from formulating answers to the questions of Japanese interlocutors is to ask some of your own.

What kind of work do you do?
Oshigoto wa nan desuka?
お仕事は何ですか？

What company do you work for?
Dokono kaisha ni otsutome desuka?
どこの会社にお勤めですか？

Are you a student?
Gakusei desuka?
学生ですか？

Where do you go to school?
Dokono gakusei desuka?
どこの学生ですか？

What do you study?
Senkō wa nan desuka?
専攻は何ですか？

What kind of work do you plan to do?
Donna shigoto o shitai desuka?
どんな仕事をしたいですか？

What are you interested in?
Nani ni kyōmi o omochi desuka?
何に興味をお持ちですか？

What do like to do in your free time?
Yasumi no hi ni wa nani o shite imasuka?
休みの日には何をしていますか？

Japanese are avid fans of sports, music, and movies, and are often surprisingly well-informed about events and trends in these areas in the West.

Do you like movies?
Eiga wa suki desuka?
映画は好きですか？

What kind of movies do you like?
Donna eiga ga suki desuka?
どんな映画が好きですか？

What's your favorite movie?
Ichiban suki na eiga wa nan desuka?
一番好きな映画は何ですか？

Who's your favorite actor?
Ichiban suki na eiga haiyū wa dare desuka?
一番好きな映画俳優は誰ですか？

Who's your favorite actress?
Ichiban suki na eiga joyū wa dare desuka?
一番好きな映画女優は誰ですか？

Do you like sports?
Supōtsu wa suki desuka?
スポーツはすきですか？

Which sports do you like?
Donna supōtsu ga suki desuka?
どんなスポーツが好きですか？

Do you play any sports?
Nanika supōtsu o shimasuka?
何かスポーツをしますか？

In judging what questions are appropriate you can be guided by the rules of decorum of your own culture (although, as noted, you may find the Japanese get very personal when using English).

What kind of books do you like?
Donna hon o yomaremasuka?
どんな本を読まれますか？

Have you ever read [AUTHOR]?
[AUTHOR] no hon o yonda koto ga arimasuka?
[著者]の本を読んだ事がありますか？

Do you like music?
Ongaku wa suki desuka?
音楽は好きですか？

What kind of music do you like?
Donna ongaku ga suki desuka?
どんな音楽が好きですか？

Who's your favorite singer?
Ichiban suki na kashu wa dare desuka?
一番好きな歌手は誰ですか？

What's your favorite musical group?
Ichiban suki na ongaku gurūpu wa dore desuka?
一番好きな音楽グループはどれですか？

Do you play any musical instruments?
Nanika gakki o ensō shimasuka?
何か楽器を演奏しますか？

Which instrument do you play?
Nanno gakki desuka?
何の楽器ですか？

Most Japanese are interested in foreign travel, even if they have never had the chance to go anywhere. Popular destinations are Europe, Australia, Hawaii, and the U.S. and Canadian West.

Have you ever traveled abroad?
Kaigai ryokō ni itta koto ga arimasuka?
海外旅行に行った事がありますか？

Which countries did you visit?
Dokono kuni ni ikimashitaka?
どこの国に行きましたか？

Did you have a good time?
Tanoshikatta desuka?
楽しかったですか？

What did you find most interesting?
Ichiban kyōmi o hikareta koto wa nan desuka?
一番興味を引かれた事は何ですか？

How was the food?
Tabemono wa ikaga deshitaka?
食べ物はいかがでしたか？

How were the people?
Sokono hitotachi wa dō deshitaka?
そこの人達はどうでしたか？

Would you like to go back again?
Mō ichido itte mitai desuka?
もう一度行ってみたいですか？

Where would you most like to travel to?
Dokoni ichiban itte mitai to omoimasuka?
どこに一番行ってみたいと思いますか？

If you happen to get into a conversation while traveling to a place you have never been, remember that this is the time to get any questions answered. English guidebooks on Japan are notoriously sketchy on all but the major cities.

Have you ever been to [PLACE]?
[PLACE] ni itta koto ga arimasuka?
［地名］に行った事がありますか？

What's it like?
Soko wa donna yōsu deshitaka?
そこはどんな様子でしたか？

What are some interesting things to do there?
Sokode nani o shitara omoshiroi desuka?
そこで何をしたらおもしろいですか？

What are the important sights to see there?
Kankō meisho wa arimasuka?
観光名所はありますか？

Are there any famous local products?
Tokusanbutsu wa arimasuka?
特産物はありますか？

Are there any festivals going on?
Matsuri o yatte imasuka?
祭をやっていますか？

Can you recommend a good place to stay?
Ii yado o gozonji desuka?
いい宿をご存じですか？

Are there any famous local dishes?
Meibutsu ryōri wa arimasuka?
名物料理はありますか？

If circumstances are appropriate, such as an encounter on a long-distance train, Japanese will likely offer you something to eat or drink. Refusing the first or second offer before finally accepting is appropriate, but not necessary. You may also attempt to reciprocate, although it is impossible to "out-host" Japanese on their home grounds.

Thank you.
Arigatō.
ありがとう。

I'll have some.   (Said just before eating)
Itadakimasu.
いただきます。

To your health!   (Literally "Dry glass," a toast)
Kanpai!
乾杯！

No thanks.
Mō jūbun desu.
もう充分です。

No thanks. I'm full.
Kekkō desu. Mō onaka ippai desu.
けっこうです。もうお腹いっぱいです。

Please have some of this.
Motto dōzo.
もっとどうぞ。

This is my treat.
Kore wa watashi no ogori desu.
これは私のおごりです。

The first several expressions below are more often used by Japanese to show polite interest in what the speaker is saying than for their literal meanings, so you may hear them quite often.

That's so, isn't it.
Sō desu ne.
そうですね。

Is that so? . . . Really?
Sō desu ka? . . . Honto ni?
そうですか？ … ほんとに？

Please say that again.
Mō ichido itte kudasai.
もう一度言ってください。

Please speak more slowly.
Yukkuri hanashite kudasai.
ゆっくり話してください。

Can you say that in English?
Sore o Eigo de itte moraemasuka?
それを英語で言ってもらえますか？

Can you translate for me?
Tsūyaku shite moraemasuka?
通訳してもらえますか？

Sorry, I only speak a little Japanese.
Sumimasen, Nihongo wa sukoshi dake dekimasu.
すみません、日本語は少しだけ出来ます。

Sorry, I don't speak Japanese.
Sumimasen, Nihongo ga zenzen dekimasen.
すみません、日本語が全然出来ません。

All conversations must eventually come to an end. Keep in mind that offers to follow-up on new friendships, even when accompanied by exchanges of addresses and elaborate farewell gestures, should be considered more a formality than substantive.

Sorry, I've got to go.
Gomennasai, dekakeru tokoro ga arimasunode.
ごめんなさい、出掛ける所がありますので。

Excuse me, I have some work to do.
Sumimasen, yō ga arimasunode.
すみません、用がありますので。

This is my stop.
Watashi wa kokode orimasu.
私はここで降ります。

Nice meeting you.
Oaidekite tanoshikatta desu.
お会い出来て楽しかったです。

Here's my address.
Kore ga watashi no jūsho desu.
これが私の住所です。

If you come to [PLACE] please look me up.
Moshi [PLACE] ni koraretara otachiyori kudasai.
もし［場所］に来られたらお立ち寄り下さい。

Until next time then.
Mata oaishimashō.
またお会いしましょう。

Goodbye.
Sayonara.
さよなら。

Conversational Tactics

Visitors will notice that casual conversation seems to take place much more readily when Japanese feel it is appropriate, that is, in their leisure hours—whether at drinking establishments, resort hotels, or vacation spots. The office worker who would not give a stranger the time of day on city streets will call out *Konnichiwa!* as you pass him on a hiking trail; the old lady who might ignore your question on the subway will want to chat with you on a long-distance train. Of course, a propensity for social engagement in idle hours is universal, but the Japanese seem epitomize this trait, appearing to outsiders somewhat taciturn at work, and garrulous at play.

• Although all Japanese study English in school, the curriculum is oriented toward reading comprehension and mastering grammar rules for the purpose of passing written examinations; thus most Japanese are not proficient conversationalists in English. However, they will likely be able to handle the simple information exchange required to get acquainted, and you may find yourself in a bilingual conversation in which you are speaking Japanese and the Japanese are speaking English. In spite of the limitations this ironic turnabout imposes, it is surprising how long and how intricate such conversations can become.

• Remember that Japanese are often embarrassed about their English proficiency, in spite of the fact that you seem unashamed of your bad Japanese, and thus may be reluctant to speak with you even under the right circumstances.

• In Japanese, your English name will "katakanized," that is, rendered into the syllabary commonly employed to transcribe foreign words and phrases. Thus "Fred" will be rendered "Furedo"; "Alice" will become "Arisu." Learning how to introduce yourself by this Japanized version of your name will help new Japanese acquaintances to remember it. It will also be the form that appears on the Japanese side of a bilingual *meishi* (name card), a must for the visitor on business.

• A few remarks about Japanese body language may be useful. Perhaps in reaction to the reduced personal space available in a crowded country, Japanese tend to guard theirs carefully; expressions of friendliness such a hug or an arm over the shoulder of a casual acquaintance may cause discomfort. When Japanese are forced to adjust to closer quarters than they would prefer, such as on crowded subways, they tend to avert their gaze as if pretending those bodies squeezed against them did not exist. In fact, direct eye contact in general is not regarded as a sign of sincerity or earnestness as it is in the West; on the contrary, it may be interpreted as bullying if one is trying to solicit agreement in an argument or business negotiations.

Getting Fed

In spite of their ongoing love affair with sushi, most Westerners remain unaware of the wide variety of ingredients and cooking styles that Japanese cuisine encompasses. This chapter contains the words and phrases you will need to enjoy delicious, representative dishes of the main types of cuisine, as well the language needed for reserving a table, ordering dishes, and settling your bill.

Restaurants and Cooking Styles

Most Japanese restaurants are small establishments specializing in a particular cooking style or ingredients. Following is a list of restaurants whose specialties you may wish to try.

fugu-ya ふぐ屋 (p. 119)
This restaurant features dishes based on the *fugu*, or blowfish, a creature with organs so poisonous that the chef who prepares the dishes must possess a special license.

kushiyaki-ya 串焼屋 (p. 118)
Skewered, breaded, and grilled offerings include meat (pork, beef, and chicken), as well as seafood and vegetables.

kushiage-ya 串揚屋 (p. 118)
Specializes in a variant of *kushiyaki*, above, with the skewered items deep-fried instead of grilled.

robatayaki-ya ろばた焼屋 (pp. 122–123)
A restaurant interpretation of "farmhouse-style" cooking, with a variety of fish and vegetables grilled over an open flame. Salads and side dishes may also be offered.

shabu shabu-ya しゃぶしゃぶ屋 (p. 125)
Patrons cook thin slices of beef and a variety of vegetables in a hot broth, dipping them in soy- or lemon-based sauces before eating. The name of this dish, *shabu shabu*, supposedly derives from the bubbling sound of the broth.

soba-ya 蕎麦屋 (p. 111)
Specializes in *soba*, buckwheat noodles, which may be served in a variety of ways.

sushi-ya 寿司屋 (pp. 112–113)
Vistors familiar with the Tokyo-style sushi best known in the West might wish to try Osaka-style sushi, for which boiled or marinated fish is laid over rice in large molds, and then sliced into servings.

tenpura-ya 天麩羅屋 (p. 110)
Seasonal vegetables, fish, and shellfish are served lightly battered and deep-fried, a cooking style borrowed from fifteenth-century Portuguese visitors to Japan.

teppanyaki-ya 鉄板焼屋 (p. 117)
The Japanese equivalent of a steakhouse, featuring sliced cuts of beef, with vegetables and sometimes seafood, cooked on a griddle in front of diners.

tonkatsu-ya 豚カツ屋 (p. 114)

The specialty here is *tonkatsu,* a tender, breaded pork cutlet, served with rice, *miso* (bean paste) soup, shredded cabbage, and pickles. Deep-fried shrimp or *korokke* (from "croquette") may be substituted for the pork.

unagi-ya うなぎ屋 (p. 119)

Boneless fillets of eel, *unagi,* are gilled over charcoal while basted with a sweet sauce, then served with rice, clear soup, and pickles.

yakitori-ya 焼鳥屋 (p. 115)

Skewered and grilled chunks of chicken are served, as well as grilled vegetables and salads.

ryotei 料亭

These traditional Japanese inn restaurants usually serve *kaiseki*, the elegantly prepared small dishes associated with the tea ceremony. As these dishes are not ordered a la carte, but served in set courses featuring seasonal ingredients, they are not listed here.

Many of the dishes served in these specialty restaurants are also available in general restaurants. The most popular of these is the *izakaya*, actually a pub in which a wide variety of dishes are served. *Izakaya* are popular drinking spots after work, and are quite bustling and noisy by Western dining standards.

In addition to Japanese food, Japanese diners are fond of the cuisines of their Asian neighbors, which they have modified somewhat to suit their own tastes. The *Chuka ryori-ya*, or Chinese restaurant, features Chinese-style stir-fried dishes over rice or noodles, soup-and-noodle dishes, and fried dumplings. The *yakiniku-ya* features Korean-style barbecue —— cuts of beef and beef parts, and vegetables, cooked by customers at their tables. Indian food has been popular with Japanese for many years, while restaurants featuring other Asian cuisines — Thai, Vietnamese, Cambodian, and Indonesian — are opening in larger cities with increasing frequency.

And, of course, Japanese eat Western foods. Their favorites include gourmet French and Italian, available in large cities, as well as fast foods from franchises such as Kentucky Fried Chicken, McDonald's, and Pizza Hut. Popular Western dishes, and variants of them, may also be found in large restaurants called *shokudō* and in *famirri resutoran* ("family restaurants") that are found in and around airports and train stations. Note that most Japanized Western foods are usually assessed as less that satisfactory by visitors seeking a taste of home.

As the best dishes are naturally served in restaurants that specialize in them, it is a good idea first to choose the style of cuisine you wish to try, then get a recommendation from a knowledgable source.

Is there a good *soba* restaurant nearby?
Kono chikaku de oishi soba-ya wa arimasuka?
この近くでおいしい蕎麦屋はありますか？

| teppanyaki restaurant | *teppanyaki-ya* | 鉄板焼屋 |
| Chinese food restaurant | *Chuka ryori-ya* | 中華料理屋 |

I'd like to eat sushi.
Sushi ga tabetai no desuga.
寿司が食べたいのですが。

| tempura | *tenpura* | 天婦羅 |
| grilled chicken | *yakitori* | 焼鳥 |

I like seafood.
Shiifūdo ga suki desu.
シーフードが好きです。

| beef | *biifu* | ビーフ |
| vegetables | *yasai* | 野菜 |

I can't eat raw seafood.
Namazakana wa taberaremasen.
生魚は食べられません。

| pork | *buta* | 豚 |
| oily foods | *aburakkoimono* | 脂っこい物 |

Is there anyplace that serves Western food?
Yōshoku no mise wa arimasuka?
洋食のお店はありますか？

Is it expensive?
Takai desuka?
高いですか？

Reservations are not a traditional Japanese custom, but are taken at hotel restaurants, good Western restaurants, and tourist restaurants (which include many excellent and elegant Japanese restaurants that cater to foreigners).

Could you make a reservation for me?
Yoyaku o onegai shimasu.
予約をおねがいします。

I'd like to make a reservation for tonight.
Konban *no yoyaku wa dekimasuka?*
今晩の予約は出来ますか？   (TIME, p. 25)

8:00 tomorrow night	*ashita no yoru hachiji*	
	明日の晩8時	(HOURS, p. 26)
7:30 Saturday night	*Doyōbi no yoru shichiji han*	
	土曜日の晩7時半	(DAYS p. 28)

I'd like a table for two people.   (COUNTERS, p. 22)
Futari *no yoyaku o shitai no desuga.*
2人の予約をしたいのですが。

four	*yonin*	4人
six	*rokunin*	6人

Do you have a no-smoking table?
Kinen tēburu wa arimasuka?
禁煙テーブルはありますか？

Do you take Diner's Club?
Daināsu kādo *wa tsukaemasuka?*
ダイナース・カードは使えますか？

American Express	*Amerikan Ekusupuresu*	
	アメリカン・エクスプレス	
Visa	*Biza kādo*	ビザ・カード
Mastercard	*Masutā kādo*	マスター・カード

The following expressions may be heard or used in any of the establishments listed in this chapter; those for which the Japanese appears first will be used by the restaurant staff rather than by you.

Irrashaimase!
いらっしゃいませ！
Welcome!

Nan mei sama desu ka?
何名様ですか？
How many are you?

Just me.   (COUNTERS, p. 22)
Hitori desu.
1人です。

Just the two of us.
Futari desu.
2人です。

We have a reservation for four.
Yonin de yoyaku o totte arimasu.
4人で予約を取ってあります。

Kochira e, dōzo.
こちらへどうぞ。
This way, please.

Excuse me!
Sumimasen!
すみません！

Please give us a menu.
Menyū o onegai shimasu.
メニューをお願いします。

Throughout this chapter, the two basic verbs for polite requests *(kudasai* and *onegai shimasu)* are used interchangeably. These are explained in more detail on p. 14 and p. 37. Review p. 32–35 for additional English borrowings commonly used in restaurants in Japan.

Onomimono wa nani ni shimasuka?
お飲み物は何にしますか？
What would you like to drink?

I'd like a beer.   (DRINKS, pp.106–9)
Biiru o kudasai.
ビールをください。

Nani ni nasaimasuka?
何になさいますか？
What will you have?

Okimarini narimashita?
お決まりになりましたか？
Have you decided yet?

I'd like this, please.
Kore o onegai shimasu.
これをお願いします。

I'd like that, please.
Sore o onegai shimasu.
それをお願いします。

May I have a fork, please?
Fōku o kudasdi.
フォークをください。

May I have a knife and fork, please?
Naifu to fōku o kudasai.
ナイフとフォークをください。

Since Japanese cuisine typically reflects seasonal offerings, it is generally a good idea to get recommendations, rather than insist upon some particular item.

Is there a set meal?
Teishoku arimasuka?
定食ありますか？

What kind of set meals are there?
Nan no teishoku ga arimasuka?
何の定食がありますか？

Is there a set meal with grilled fish?
Sakanayaki *teishoku ga arimasuka?*
魚焼き定食がありますか？

sushi	*sushi*	寿司
tempura	*tenpura*	天婦羅

What special dishes do you have today?
Kyō no higawari wa nan desuka?
今日の日替りは何ですか？

What do you recommend?
Osusumehin wa nan desuka?
おすすめ品は何ですか？

It's delicious.
Oishii desu.
おいしいです。

It has an interesting flavor.
Chinmi desu.
珍味です。

I really don't care for it.
Amari suki dewa arimasen.
あまり好きではありません。

Itadakimasu, literally "I humbly accept (what is offered)" is said before starting to eat; *gochisōsama* is said in thanks upon finishing a meal, either to your hosts or to restaurant staff. The "Fingertips" at the end of this chapter contain additional useful information about Japanese dining etiquette.

Let's eat!
Itadakimasu!
いただきます！

May I have more of this?
Kore o mō sukosi itadakemasuka?
これをもう少しいただけますか？

No more for me. I'm full.
Watashi wa jūbun desu. Onaka ga ippai desu.
私は充分です。お腹がいっぱいです。

May we have the check?
Okanjō onegai shimasu.
お勘定お願いします。

Can we have separate checks?
Okanjō o betsubetsu ni shite kudasai.
お勘定を別々にして下さい。

Can I use this credit card?
Kono kurejitto kādo o tsukaemasuka?
このクレジット・カードを使えますか？

May I have a receipt, please?
Ryōshūsho o itadakemasuka?
領収書をいただけますか？

Thanks for the meal!
Gochisōsama!
ごちそうさま！

In Japan the *kissaten*, or coffee shop, is a ubiquitous institution that features tea, fruit drinks, and light refreshments as well as coffee. It is expected that patrons will linger to relax, talk, or read. Note that *burendo*, or blended coffee, is used to refer to a stronger brew, while *Amerikan kōhii*, "American coffee," is used to refer to weaker coffee.

Do you have expresso?
Esupuresso arimasuka?
エスプレッソありますか？

I'd like a blended coffee.
Burendo kōhii *onegai shimasu.*
ブレンド・コーヒーお願いします。

regular coffee	*Amerikan kōhii*
	アメリカン・コーヒー
cafe au lait	*kafe ore*
	カフェ・オ・レ
mocha blend	*moka burendo*
	モカ・ブレンド
ice coffee	*aisu kōhii*
	アイス・コーヒー
ice tea	*aisu tii*
	アイス・ティー
tea with milk	*miruku tii*
	ミルク・ティー
tea with lemon	*remon tii*
	レモン・ティー
hot chocolate	*kokoa*
	ココア

"Juice" *(jūsu)* in Japan may be carbonated and contain little or no real fruit juice; it is typically more like what Americans call "soda."

Do you have ginger ale?
Jinjā ēru arimasuka?
ジンジャー・エールありますか？

I'd like tomato juice.
Tomato jūsu onegai shimasu.
トマト・ジュースお願いします。

orange juice	*orenji jūsu*	オレンジ・ジュース
banana juice	*banana jūsu*	バナナ・ジュース
cream soda	*kuriimu sōda*	クリーム・ソーダ
cola	*kōra*	コーラ
milk	*miruku*	ミルク
club soda	*kurabu sōda*	クラブ・ソーダ
tonic water	*tonikku uōtā*	トニック・ウォーター
mineral water	*mineraru uōtā*	ミネラル・ウォーター
cold water	*ohiya*	お冷

banana yoghurt drink *banana yōguruto dorinku*
バナナ・ヨーグルト・ドリンク

strawberry yoghurt drink *sutoroberii yōguruto dorinku*
ストロベリー・ヨーグルト・ドリンク

orange yoghurt drink *orenji yōguruto dorinku*
オレンジ・ヨーグルト・ドリンク

Wine, liquor, and mixed drinks are usually served only in Western-style bars and restaurants, while Japanese-style drinking establishments typically offer only beer, sake, and *shōchū*. This latter is a clear grain or vegetable distillate that is drunk with a mixer such as fruit juice, a concoction called a *chūhai*, short for "*shōchū* highball."

Do you have any dark beer?
Kuro biiru arimasuka?
黒ビールありますか？

imported beer	*gaikoku no biiru*	外国のビール
draft beer	*nama biiru*	生ビール

I'll have a beer.
Biiru o kudasai.
ビールお願いします。

large draft beer	*nama biiru no dai*	生ビールの大
regular draft beer	*nama biiru no chū*	生ビールの中
small draft beer	*nama biiru no shō*	生ビールの小

I'll have sake.
Nibonshu onegai shimasu.
日本酒お願いします。

hot sake	*atsukan*	あつかん
cold sake	*hiyazake*	冷酒

shōchū on the rocks.   *shōchū no on za rokku*
ショーチュウのオンザロック

shōchū with lemon soda   *shōchū no remon sodawari*
ショーチュウのレモンソーダ割

shōchū with lime soda   *shōchū no raimu sodawari*
ショーチュウのライムソーダ割

shōchū with Oolong tea   *shōchū no Urōncha wari*
ショーチュウのウーロン茶割

Note that Japanese prefer their whiskey and water
(mizuwari) very watery, and real draft beer (from
kegs) is normally available only in the summer.

Do you have red wine?
Aka wain arimasuka?
赤ワインありますか？

| white wine | *shiro wain* | 白ワイン |
| rose | *roze* | ロゼ |

A glass (of wine), please.
Gurasu wain onegai shimasu.
グラスワインお願いします。

| half-bottle | *bāfu botoru* | ハーフ・ボトル |
| bottle | *botoru* | ボトル |

I'll have scotch.
Sukotchi uisukii onegai shimasu.
スコッチ・ウイスキーお願いします。

bourbon	*bābon*	バーボン
vodka	*uokka*	ウォッカ
gin	*jin*	ジン

On the rocks, please.
On za rokku ni shite kudasai.
オンザロックにして下さい。

with soda	*sōdawari*	ソーダ割
with water	*mizuwari*	水割
straight	*sutorēto*	ストレート

At the *tenpura-ya*, it is best to sit at the counter, so these delicious batter-fried morsels will be served to you fresh and hot. The fish and vegetables served at a good tempura shop will be those in season.

I'd like the tempura selection.
***Tenpura moriawase** onegai shimasu.*
天婦羅盛り合わせお願いします。

mixed vegetables	*yasai tenpura moriawase*
	野菜天婦羅盛り合わせ
seasonal vegetables	*kisetsu yasai tenpura moriawase*
	季節野菜天婦羅盛り合わせ

I'd like shitake mushrooms.
***Shiitake** onegai shimasu.*
しいたけお願いします。

eggplant	*nasu*	なす
bell pepper	*piiman*	ピーマン
asparagus	*asupara*	アスパラ
carrot	*ninjin*	人参
chrysanthemum leaf	*shungiku*	春菊
sweet potato	*satsuma imo*	さつまいも
squid	*ika*	いか
shrimp	*ebi*	えび
eel	*anago*	あなご
smelt	*wakasagi*	わかさぎ
sillago (fish)	*kisu*	きす
scallop	*hotate gai*	帆立貝
giant prawn	*kuruma ebi*	車えび

Noodle lovers will enjoy the thin, buckwheat noodles called *soba,* or the thicker wheat noodles called *udon.* These are served in a soy-based broth and can be topped with a variety of ingredients.

I'd like the plain *soba.*
Kake soba o kudasai.
かけそばをください。

soba with tempura	*tenpura soba*	天婦羅そば
seaweed	*wakame soba*	ワカメそば
fried tofu	*kitsune soba*	きつねそば
mountain vegetables	*sansai soba*	山菜そば
mushrooms	*nameko soba*	なめこそば
herring	*nishin soba*	にしんそば
cold, plain soba	*zaru soba*	ざるそば

I'd like *udon* with deep-fried prawns and vegetables.
Tenpura udon *onegai shimasu.*
天婦羅うどんお願いします。

seaweed	*wakame udon*	わかめうどん
fried tofu	*kitsune udon*	きつねうどん
mountain vegetables	*sansai udon*	山菜うどん
mushrooms	*nameko*	なめこうどん
herring	*nishin udon*	にしんうどん
the mixed udon pot	*nabeyaki udon*	鍋焼きうどん

Although it is possible to run up a hefty bill ordering by the piece at a good sushi shop, a set meal, or *teishoku*, can be a real bargain; however, these will normally be available only at lunchtime. Note that sushi shops have their own special words for such common items as soy sauce and tea.

I'd like the *nigiri* assortment.
Nigiri ichininmae onegai shimasu.
にぎり一人前お願いします。

large nigiri assortment	*nigiri omori o ichininmae* にぎり大盛りを一人前
least expensive assortment	*nigiri no nami o ichininmae* にぎりの並を一人前
mid-range assortment	*nigiri no chū o ichininmae* にぎりの中を一人前
top-class assortment	*nigiri no jō o ichininmae* にぎりの上を一人前

I'd like a tuna roll.
Tekkamaki onegai shimasu.
てっか巻お願いします。

pickle roll	*oshinko maki*	おしんこ巻
cucumber roll	*kappa maki*	かっぱ巻
mixed sashimi over rice	*chirashi zushi*	ちらし寿司

May I have some tea?
Agari o kudasai.
あがりをください。

soy sauce	*murasaki*	むらさき
pickled ginger	*gari*	がり
horseradish	*wasabi*	山葵

The Tokyo style of sushi, known as *nigiri zushi*, is most familiar to Westerners, although you migh wish to to try the Osaka style, *oshi zushi,* during your visit. Remember, you don't need to know the names of all the fish; you can simply sit at the counter and point.

I'd like horse mackerel.
Aji o onegai shimasu.
あじをお願いします。

young yellowtail	*hamachi*	はまち
yellowtail	*buri*	ぶり
tuna	*maguro*	まぐろ
conger eel	*anago*	あなご
sole	*hirame*	ひらめ
sardine	*iwashi*	いわし
marinated sardine	*kohada*	こはだ
shrimp	*ebi*	えび
mantis shrimp	*shako*	しゃこ
squid	*ika*	いか
octopus	*tako*	たこ
clam	*hamaguri*	はまぐり
abalone	*awabi*	あわび
round clam	*aoyagi*	青柳
scallop	*hotate gai*	帆立貝
cockle	*tori gai*	とり貝
ark shell	*aka gai*	赤貝
sea urchin eggs	*uni*	うに
salmon eggs	*ikura*	いくら

No horseradish, please.
Wasabi nuki de onegai shimasu.
山葵ぬきでお願いします。

Although specializing in cuts of pork, other main dishes are offered in a *tonkatsu-ya*. Here the *teishoku*, or set meal, is a filling lunchtime bargain, offering the selected main dish accompanied by rice, *miso* soup, a grated cabbage salad, and pickles.

I'd like to have the set meal.
Teishoku de onegai shimasu.
定食でお願いします。

I'd like the pork cutlet.
Ton katsu o kudasai.
トンカツをください。

top-grade cutlet	*hire katsu*	ヒレカツ
chicken cutlet	*chikin katsu*	チキンカツ
fried prawns	*ebi furai*	エビフライ
fried oysters	*kaki furai*	カキフライ
potato croquette	*poteto korokke*	ポテトコロッケ
crab croquette	*kani korokke*	カニコロッケ
salmon croquette	*sāmon korokke*	サーモンコロッケ
skewered cutlet	*kushi katsu*	串カツ
fried horse mackerel	*aji furai*	アジフライ
cutlet with cheese	*chizu katsu*	チーズカツ
minced pork cake	*menchi katsu*	メンチカツ
cutlet on rice	*katsu don*	カツドン

I'd like some salad.
Sarada onegai shimasu.
野菜サラダお願いします。

pickles	*oshinko*	おしんこ
soybean-paste soup	*miso shiru*	味噌汁
rice	*raisu*	ライス
bonito broth	*osumashi*	おすまし
mushroom soup	*namekojiru*	なめこ汁

Since the main offering is chicken grilled on skewers, most Westerners are comfortable with *yakitori-ya*. Note that these are chiefly drinking establishments, and may offer many of the dishes found in *izakaya* (p. 122), including grilled vegetables and salads. You can specify that your chicken be cooked *shio* (salted), or *tare* (after dipping in a sweet sauce).

I'd like a skewer of skinless breast pieces.
Sasami o kudasai.
ささみをください。

boneless pieces with skin	*shōniku*	しょうにく
minced chicken meatballs	*tsukune*	つくね
chicken with spring onion	*hasami*	はさみ

Two skewers, please.   (COUNTERS, p. 23)
Nihon kudasai.
二本ください。

Cooked with salt, please.
Shio yaki de onegai shimasu.
塩焼きでお願いします。

Cooked with sauce, please.
Tare yaki de onegai shimau.
タレ焼きでお願いします。

I'd like grilled chicken wings.
Tebasaki onegai shimasu.
手羽先お願いします。

liver	*rebā*	レバー
gizzards	*sunagimo*	砂肝
legs	*momo*	もも
mushrooms	*shiitake*	しいたけ
bell pepper	*piiman*	ピーマン
spring onion	*naganegi*	長ねぎ

Diners cook this pancake-like dish themselves on a solid grill (*teppan*) set into the table. The basic dough mixed with selected ingredients is poured on the grill, turned when brown, and basted with a sweet brown sauce. It can be topped with condiments or an egg prior to eating. Fried noodles are also a popular dish here.

I'd like beef *okonomiyaki* style.
Biifu no okonomiyaki o onegai shimasu.
ビーフのお好み焼きをお願いします。

pork	*buta*	豚
shrimp	*ebi*	エビ
oysters	*kaki*	カキ
squid	*ika*	いか
mixed	*okonomiyaki mikkusu*	ミックス
deluxe mixed	*derakksu mikkusu*	
	デラックス・ミックス	

I'd like that *okonomiyaki* style with egg.
Okonomiyaki o tsukimi de onegai shimasu.
お好み焼きを月見でお願いします。

I'd like fried *soba* noodles.
Yakisoba o kudasai.
焼きソバをください。

I'd like fried *udon* noodles.
Yakiudon o onegai shimasu.
焼きウドンをお願いします。

This up-scale variant of *teppan* cooking features steaks, seafood, and vegetables lightly grilled by the chef in front of diners, often accompanied by skillful flourishes of ingredients and utensils (as popularized in the West by the Benihana chain). Note that some of these dishes you can cook yourself at an *okonimiyaki* restaurant; likewise, many *teppanyaki* places offer *okonomiyaki*.

I'd like the fillet steak.
Hire sutēki o onegai shimasu.
ヒレ・ステーキをお願いします。

sirloin steak	*sāroin sutēki*	
	サーロイン・ステーキ	
tenderloin steak	*tendāroin sutēki*	
	テンダーロイン・ステーキ	
beef tongue	*gyū tan*	牛タン
pork	*pōku*	ポーク
scallops	*hotate gai*	帆立
prawns	*ebi*	エビ
squid	*ika*	イカ
mixed grill	*mikkusu guriru*	ミックス・グリル
potatoes	*poteto*	ポテト
bean curd	*tōfu sutēki*	トーフ・ステーキ
bean sprouts	*moyashi batā*	モヤシ・バター
eggplant	*nasu batā*	ナス・バター
mushrooms	*shiitake batā*	しいたけ・バター
seasonal vegetables	*kisetsu yasai no moriawase*	
	季節野菜の盛りあわせ	

At a *kushiyaki-ya*, skewered tidbits are cooked on an open grill, while at a *kushiage-ya* they are deep fried. Either dish may served in *izakaya* and other restaurants, while in establishments that specialize in them, they often serve as snacks to accompany drinking and high-level business entertainment, with prices reflecting this function. Finished skewers are often placed in a pottery jar and counted to determine the final bill.

I'd like a skewer of pork.
Hitokuchi pōku o onegai shimasu.
一口ポークをお願いします。

beef	*biifu*	ビーフ
chicken breast	*sasami maki*	ささみまき
shrimp	*ebi*	エニ
squid	*ika*	イカ
scallops	*hotate gai*	帆立貝
bean curd	*tōfu*	豆腐
lotus root	*hasu*	はす
bell pepper	*piiman*	ピーマン
asparagus	*asupara*	アスパラ
mushrooms	*shiitake*	しいたけ
devil's tongue	*konnyaku*	こんにゃく

Although the mention of eel does not typically entice Western taste buds to salivate, few who try this delicacy dislike it. The *unagi-ya* features fresh-water eel filleted, steamed, and then grilled over charcoal, usually basted with a sweet sauce. It is considered a summer delicacy as it is thought to provide the stamina required for hot, sultry days. The *fugu-ya* serves the edible parts of the poisonous blowfish, or globefish, in a variety of ways. Due to the scarcity of chefs licenced to prepare this specialty, *fugu* restaurants are usually expensive.

I'd like skewered eel with sweet sauce.
Unagi no kabayaki *o onegai shimasu.*
うなぎのかば焼をお願いします。

skewered eel without sauce	*shirayaki*	しら焼
eel on rice in a lacquered box	*una jū*	うな重
eel over rice in a bowl	*unadon*	うなどん
clear soup with eel liver	*kimosui*	肝吸
the set meal	*teishoku*	定食

I'd like sliced raw blowfish.
Fugu sashi *o kudasai.*
ふぐさしをください。

blowfish stew with vegetables	*fugu chiri*
	ふぐちり
blowfish stew with rice	*fugu zōsui*
	ふぐぞうすい
blowfish fin in rice wine	*hire zake*
	ひれ酒

The Japanese stew called *oden* is found in some restaurants and convenience stores, but it is most often eaten outside, on chairs and tables surrounding the one-man vending carts from which it is served. You can select which items in the mix you prefer. The sweet-potato vendor drives through the neighborhoods hawking his offerings, while fried noodles and *takoyaki* (an octopus and vegetable dumpling) are sold from booths set up at festivals and other events.

I'll have a mixed platter of *oden*.
Oden o hito sara kudasai.
おでんを一皿ください。

I'll have the grilled beancurd.
Yakidofu o kudasai.
焼豆腐をください。

stuffed beancurd	*fukubukuro*	ふく袋
fish paste tube	*chikuwa*	ちくわ
radish	*daikon*	大根
kelp	*konbu*	コブ
minced chicken ball	*tsukune*	つくね
stuffed cabbage	*rōru kyabetsu*	ロールキャベツ
hard-boiled egg	*tamago*	玉子

One sweet potato, please.   (COUNTERS, p. 22)
Yaki imo ikko onegai shimasu.
焼イモを一個お願いします。

Fried noodles, please.
Yakisoba o kudasai.
焼ソバをください。

Takoyaki, please.
Takoyaki o kudasai.
タコ焼をください。

Boxed lunches to take out, called *bentō*, can be found in department stores and at take-out windows in and around train stations. Main dishes are usually accompanied by rice, vegetables, and pickles.

I'll have a fish and seaweed box lunch.
Nori bentō o kudasai.
のり弁当をください。

grilled salmon	*sake bentō*	シャケ弁当
grilled meat	*yakiniku bentō*	焼肉弁当
grilled beef patty	*hanbāgu bentō*	ハンバーグ弁当
chicken and egg	*soboro bentō*	そぼろ弁当
grilled eel	*unagi bentō*	うなぎ弁当
mountain vegetable	*sansai bentō*	山菜弁当
fried squid	*ika furai bentō*	イカフライ弁当
fried horse mackerel	*aji furai bentō*	アジフライ弁当
fried chicken	*kara age bentō*	唐揚げ弁当
fried shrimp	*ebi furai bentō*	エビフライ弁当
fried pork cutlet	*tonkatsu bentō*	トンカツ弁当
deluxe box lunch	*makunuochi bentō*	幕の内弁当

I'll have this one.
Kore o kudasai.
これをください。

I'd like soybean soup with that.
Miso shiru o kudasai.
味噌汁をください。

I'd like an Oolong tea, please.
Uroncha o kudasai.
ウーロン茶をください。

An *izakaya* is more a pub than a restaurant, but since the custom in Japan is always to eat when drinking and socializing, a wide variety of small dishes can be ordered. Many of these dishes are served in the other restaurants listed, and many dishes listed under those restaurants may also be ordered at the *izakaya*.

What grilled fish is good today?
Nanika oishii yakizakana wa arimasuka?
何かおいしい焼魚はありますか？

What vegetables are good today?
Kyō no osusume yasai wa nan desuka?
今日のおすすめ野菜は何ですか？

We'd like to try some of today's special dishes.
Kyō no osusumehin o onegai shimasu.
今日のおすすめ品をお願いします。

Green salad, please.
Guriin sarada o onegai shimasu.
グリーンサラダをお願いします。

tomato salad	*tomato sarada*	トマトサラダ
Japanese-style salad	*wafū sarada*	和風サラダ
seaweed salad	*kaisō sarada*	海草サラダ
tuna salad	*tsuna sarada*	ツナサラダ
soup with mushrooms	*nameko jiru*	なめこ汁
soup with seaweed	*wakame jiru*	ワカメ汁
soup with bean curd	*tofu jiru*	豆腐汁
pork and potato stew	*nikku jaga*	肉じゃが
corn sauteed in butter	*kōn batā*	コーンバター
boiled soybeans	*edamame*	枝豆

A *robatayaki* might be described as an up-scale *izakaya,* featuring visible central grills that patrons sit around. With its emphasis on seafood, this is the perfect restaurant for fish lovers who are not thrilled with sushi. Since diners sit in full view of the best of the day's offerings, one need not learn the names of all the fish and vegetables——simply point and request.

I'd like grilled trout.
Masu o onegai shimasu.
ますをお願いします。

herring	*nishin*	にしん
mackerel	*saba*	さば
mackerel pike	*sanma*	さんま
atka mackerel	*hokke*	ほっけ
chicken	*yakitori*	焼鳥
bacon and asparagus	*aspara bēkon*	アスパラベーコン
eggplant	*nasu*	茄子
mushrooms	*shiitake*	しいたけ
bell pepper	*piiman*	ピーマン
gingko nuts	*ginnan*	ぎんなん
potatoes	*jagaimo*	じゃがいも
corn on the cob	*tōmorokoshi*	とうもろこし

I'd like the deep-fried squid legs.
Geso age o onegai shimasu.
ゲソ揚げをお願いします。

fried tofu	*atsu age*	厚あげ
fried chicken	*kara age*	鳥の唐揚げ
fried potatoes	*potato furai*	ポテトフライ
fried dumplings	*age gyōza*	揚げギョーザ

Japanese enjoy a huge variety of rice dishes, which may be offered at several of the restaurants described in this chapter. These range from grilled or stuffed rice-ball snacks *(onigiri)* to "filler" dishes such as tea or broth poured over rice *(chazuke)* to complete one-dish meals of rice mixed and steamed or topped with other ingredients *(kamameishi* and *donburi).*

I'll have the pickled plum "rice ball."
***Umeboshi** no onigiri o onegai shimasu.*
うめぼしのおにぎりをお願いします。

cod roe	*tarako*	たらこ
salmon	*shake*	しゃけ
plain grilled	*yaki onigiri*	焼きおにぎり

I'll have the rice in tea with pickles.
***Tsukemono** chazuke o kudasai.*
漬け物茶漬をください。

seaweed	*nori chazuke*	のり茶漬
salmon	*sake chazuke*	さけ茶漬
cod roe	*tarako chazuke*	たらこ茶漬

I'll have the "rice pot" with salmon.
***Sake** kamameshi o onegai shimasu.*
さけ釜めしをお願いします。

crab	*kani*	カニ釜めし
oysters	*kaki*	カキ釜めし
cod and vegetables	*sansai*	山菜釜めし
chicken	*tori*	鳥釜めし
mixed	*gomoku*	五目釜めし

I'll have the pork and onion over rice.
***Katsudon** o kudasai.*
カツどんをください。

tempura shrimp	*tendon*	天どん
chicken and egg	*oyakodon*	親子どん

Japan has its own delicious variants of the table-cooked stews that probably had their origins in the nomadic campfire cooking of the Asian mainland. Since these *nabe* ("pot") dishes can feature seafood, beef, pork and a variety of vegetables, there is some combination of ingredients to please every palate. These warming and surprisingly hearty wintertime meals appear on the menus of *izakaya* when the weather turns cold, while *sukiyaki* and *shabu shabu*, which feature beef, can be found year-round (and are best eaten) in restaurants that specialize in them, often the same restaurant.

I'd like the cod and vegetable stew.
***Tarachirinabe** o onegai shimasu.*
たらちり鍋をお願いします。

fish	*chirinabe*	ちり鍋
seafood and chicken	*yosenabe*	寄せ鍋
salmon and crab	*ishikarinabe*	石狩鍋
oyster	*dotenabe*	土手鍋

I'll have the *shabu shabu*.
Shabu shabu o onegai shimasu.
しゃぶしゃぶをお願いします。

I'd like the *sukiyaki*.
Sukiyaki o onegai shimasu.
すき焼をお願いします。

I'd like an order of mixed vegetables.
***Yasai moriawase** o kudasai.*
野菜盛り合わせをください。

beancurd	*tōfu*	豆腐
shrimp	*ama ebi*	甘エビ
noodles	*harusame*	はるさめ
rice	*gohan*	ごはん

Chinese food has been a staple of the Japanese diet long enough to have been modified to conform to Japanese tastes. Most Chinese restaurants in Japan thus serve dishes that are generally sweeter and less spicy than their mainland counterparts.

I'd like the spicy tofu with meat.
Mābō dōfu o onegai shimasu.
マーボー豆腐をお願いします。

sweet and sour pork	*subuta*	酢豚
shrimp and chili sauce	*ebi no chiri sōsu*	
		エビのチリソース
fried noodles	*yakisoba*	焼ソバ
cold noodle salad	*hiyashi chūka*	冷し中華
noodles in broth	*rāmen*	ラーメン
noodles in bean paste broth	*miso rāmen*	
		味噌ラーメン
noodles with pork in broth	*chāshū men*	
		チャーシューメン
plain fried rice	*chāhan*	チャーハン
shrimp fried rice	*ebi chāhan*	エビチャーハン
crab fried rice	*kani chāhan*	カニチャーハン
steamed dumplings	*shūmai*	シューマイ
fried pork dumplings	*gyōza*	餃子
mixed fried rice		*gomoku chāhan*
		五目チャーハン
meat and vegetables on rice		*chūka don*
		中華どん
noodle soup with dumplings		*wantan men*
		ワンタンメン

The *yakiniku-ya,* or "Korean barbecue" is an inexpensive answer for those who have been in the land of seafood and noodles long enough to be craving beef. Be forewarned, however, that nearly every part of the animal is offered. Since the meat and vegetables are prepared by customers on their own grill, it is great fun for a group outing.

I'll have the roast cut.
Rōsu o onegai simasu.
ロースをお願いします。

top-class roast cut	*jō rōsu*	上ロース
fatter cut	*karubi*	カルビ
heart	*hatsu yaki*	ハツ焼
liver	*rebāyaki*	レバー焼
tongue	*tan yaki*	タン焼
tripe	*mino yaki*	ミノ焼
fresh vegetable	*yasai yaki*	野菜焼
pickled cucumbers	*oi kimuchi*	オイキムチ
pickled radishes	*kakuteki*	カクテキ
pickled cabbage	*kimuchi*	キムチ
egg soup	*tamago sūpu*	玉子スープ
seaweed soup	*wakame sūpu*	ワカメスープ
beef and vegetables on rice	*bibimba* ビビンバ	
meat and vegetable soup	*kuppa* クッパ	

As with other words borrowed from Western languages,
the names of Western foods are generally rendered into
the Japanese phonetic system. Such words generally
remain recognizable to non-Japanese; "hamburger,"
for example, becomes *hanbāgā*. See "Words You
Already Know," (pp. 32–35), for more Western dishes .

I'd like a hamburger.
Hanbāgā o onegai shimasu.
ハンバーガーをお願いします。

cheeseburger	*chiizubāgā*	チーズバーガー
French fries	*Furenchi furai*	フレンチフライ
hot dog	*hotto doggu*	ホットドッグ
an omelette	*omuretsu*	オムレツ
green salad	*guriin sarada*	グリーンサラダ
corn soup	*kōn sūpu*	コーンスープ
beef stew	*biifu sichū*	ビーフシチュー

I'd like spaghetti with meat sauce.
Supagetē miitosōsu o kudasai.
スパゲッティーミートソースをください。

| mushrooms | *kinoko* | 木の子 |
| shellfish | *bongōre* | ボンゴーレ |

I'd like a pizza with mushrooms.
Mashurūmu no piza o onegai shimasu.
マッシュルームのピザをお願いします。

pepperoni	*peparoni*	ペパロニ
green peppers	*piiman*	ピーマン
onions	*onion*	オニオン

I'd like chicken curry with rice.
Chikin kāre o kudasai.
チキンカレーをください。

| beef curry | *biifu kāre* | ビーフカレー |
| seafood curry | *siifudo kāre* | シーフードカレー |

Western foods my be served anywhere from Western chain outlets (McDonald's, Kentucky Fried Chicken, and Denny's are all popular) to *kissaten* (the "coffee shop,") to the *famirii resutoran* ("family restaurant"), which might be described as a Denny's clone. Keep in mind that although the names may be exact transliterations, the dishes will not be.

I'd like the macaroni gratin.
Makaroni gratan *o onegai shimasu.*
マカロニ・グラタンをお願いします。

shrimp gratin	*ebi gratan*	エビグラタン
mushroom gratin	*kinoko gratan*	キノコグラタン

I'd like a large.
Dai de onegai shimasu.
大でお願いします。

medium	*chū*	中
small	*shō*	小

I'd like it rare.
Reā de kudasai.
レアーでください。

medium	*midiamu*	ミディアム
well done	*uerudan*	ウェルダン

I'd like ketchup.
Kechappu *o kudasai.*
ケチャップをください。

mustard	*masutādo*	マスタード
mayonnaise	*mayonēzu*	マヨネーズ
lettuce	*retasu*	レタス
tomato	*tomato*	トマト
salt	*shio*	塩
pepper	*koshō*	胡椒
dressing	*doresshingu*	ドレッシング

Eating in Japan

Japan is a wonderful country for the food lover, not because of its great number of four-star restaurants, but rather because the Japanese eat an incredibly wide variety of food items prepared in almost every manner imaginable. Where else in the world could one order *hirezaki*, the toasted fin of a poisonous globefish served in rice wine, or a tempura assortment containing *shungiku no ha*, battered and deep-fried chrysanthemum leaves?

• Japanese food is also noted for the great attention paid to presentation and to seasonal ingredients. These attributes will be most obvious in the Japanese meal you will be served at a top-class inn. Dinner here may consist of a dozen or more small dishes, affording the best chance to sample many ingredients and cooking styles.

• The *teishoku*, or set meal, of practically all restaurants are a better bargain than ordering a la carte, and quality rarely suffers. In some restaurants, particularly sushi and eel shops, a rating system is employed to distinguish the quality of the offerings. Top-class is *matsu* (松, meaning "pine"); middle-class is *take* (竹, meaning "bamboo"); while ordinary fare is *ume* (梅, meaning "plum"). These classes are sometimes indicated with *tokujō* (特上, meaning "especially superior"); *jō* (上, meaning "superior"); and *nami* (並, meaning "ordinary").

• For those with less adventurous palates, there is the *kissaten*, a coffee shop that also serves Western-style snacks such as sandwiches, spaghetti, and baked rice and noodle dishes. There are also, of course, hotel restaurants; most tourist hotels have both Japanese- and Western-style dining rooms. There are also *shokudō,* large restaurants typically found around train stations, in departments stores and office build-ing basements, and serving Japanese, Chinese, and Western dishes. These establishments usually display plastic models of the dishes they serve in a window or display case. Simply get the attention of a waiter or waitress and point to what you would like . Visitors often mistakenly assume these plastic models are displayed for their benefit and are shy about using this method of ordering. In fact, this custom originated in nine-teenth-century Japan as a way of showing Japanese what the many new dishes being introduced from the West were like.

• A lot of dauntingly misleading information has been written about Japanese manners, giving the impression that it is extremely easy to offend. In fact, in Japan as elsewhere, a strict code of etiquette govern-ing table manners has given way to a more casual and comfortable approach to dining, and one can get by on common sense and a little observation. It is true that food should not be passed from chopsticks to chop-sticks, and that chopsticks should not be placed upright in the rice, both actions reminscent of Buddhist funerary rites. Is is also true that Japanese soups and broths are slurped, although this custom indicating gustatory pleasure is more likely to offend the non-slurper than vice versa. Japanese soups, by the way, are drunk directly from the bowl, although they can be stirred a bit with chopsticks to mix contents which may have settled. As elsewhere, guests should not begin eating before the host, unless bidden.

• Drinking is an important component of Japanese business and social life, and it is always accompanied by eating. After work, especially, urban workers will head for an *izakaya* or other small establishment to drink beer or sake while sharing a variety of small dishes. These workers may have another meal, including rice or noodles, after returning home. The boisterous and friendly atmosphere of these pub-restaurants makes them a good place to begin your experimentation with Japanese cuisine. A few sincere inquiries about what is available and a few comments on the dishes enjoyed may get you not only a good dinner but some new friends as well. It is customary in Japan to pour beer for others and wait for them to pour for you, raising your glass to allow them to do so. If you continue drinking, your hosts will continue pouring, so the only way to prevent them from refilling your glass is to leave it full.

• It is frequently remarked that Japan is an expensive place to eat, and horror stories abound in the Western media of $200 steaks and even $200 melons. It is true that Japanese restrictions on imported foodstuffs can make them ludicrously expensive, but only a foreign correspondent on an expense account would be foolish enough to seek them out. Use common sense: Don't order fresh-squeezed orange juice (made from California oranges) in a hotel restaurant. Instead, satisfy your craving with some *mikan* (juicy, seedless mandarin oranges) from a local fruit stand. Don't expect that a fine Italian restaurant in Tokyo will be a good value (although the food may be quite good). For bargains, follow the Japanese, especially at lunchtime; a sushi *teishoku* then will cost about half (¥900) what it would in midtown Manhattan, and the quality of the fish will be far superior.

Getting What You Want

In spite of the high value of the yen compared to most of the world's currencies, Japan remains a shopper's paradise. This chapter contains the words and phrases you will need to find and purchase what you are looking for, whether high-tech electronic goods or traditional craft items. If you are seeking services rather than shopping for goods, see Chapter 7.

Shopping in Japan

Japan is a world-class consumer society, where customers are continually wooed with artful displays of the newest and finest goods, accompanied by service unrivaled elsewhere in the world. Moreover, Japan is the leading manufacturer of the high-tech consumer goods most sought after today, so it is the perfect place to browse and check out what is new, even if you decide to buy elsewhere. And, of course, Japan has a vast variety of traditional art and craft items that make wonderful souvenirs, as well as gifts for those back home. In Tokyo, a stop on practically all itineraries, some important shopping areas are:

Ginza 銀座
This area east of Yurakucho Station is usually what comes to mind when shopping in Japan is mentioned. It still boasts some of the largest and finest, as well as oldest, department stores in the nation, and its warren of back and side streets are crammed with shops and boutiques selling luxury goods of all types.

Akihabara 秋葉原

This area, surrounding the station of the same name, has the greatest concentration of stores selling cameras, audio and video equipment, computer and video game hardware and software, and household appliances and electronic goods of all types. It is a showcase of the latest in high-tech gadgetry, with constant displays and demonstrations, and with hands-on trials encouraged.

Kanda-Jimbocho 神田・神保町

A student area boasting more than half a dozen colleges and universities and hundreds of bookstores, this is where literary Tokyoites browse for something to read. Although most books here are in Japanese, stores such as Sanseido, Kitazawa, and Charles Tuttle sell books in English, while the second floor of Isseido carries used and rare books and maps in both English and Japanese.

Ogawamachi 小川町

Japan is now a major producer of top-quality sporting goods and accessories. These can a viewed and purchased in the many multi-story sports emporiums along Yasukuni Dori, between Jimbocho Station (convenient to the bookstore area above) and Ogawamachi Station.

Shitamachi 下町

Literally meaning "downtown," this area to the east of the center of modern Tokyo has preserved more old wooden shops selling traditional goods than other areas of the city. For those looking for something particular, a good guide will be needed (recommended is

Kites, Crackers, and Craftsmen, published by Shufunotomo). Sensoji, sometimes referred to as Asakusa Kannon temple, is one of the oldest temples in the city, and could be considered the gateway to old Tokyo. Many traditional items can be purchased along the Nakamise, the main street leading to this temple.

Harajuku 原宿
This area, especially along the tree-lined boulevard called Omote Sando, and along Meiji Dori to Shibuya, is the area in which to see Young Tokyo. Although a few stores along Omote Sando, such as the Oriental Bazaar, sell traditional goods for tourists, this is really the place to see what Japanese are assimilating from the West, and what the latest trends are in fashion, food, and pop culture.

As in the West, bargaining in Japan is not appropriate in most retail outlets, with the exception of the discount electronic stores, where one is free to ask *Sukoshi makete moraemasuka?* ("Can you give me a little better price?"). In flea markets and outdoor bazaars, of course, bargaining is the rule. Unless you are an expert, however, it might be better not to press for a deal on an expensive artwork or antique there; the extra you will pay at a reputable dealer will also purchase peace of mind.

Shopping seldom requires finely honed language skills; the desire and need to exchange money for goods is universally recognized. Thus although the literal translation for "I want to buy X" would be *X o kaitaino desuga*, the structures used here are "Do you have X?" (*X wa arimasuka?*) and "Please give me X"

(*X o kudasai*). These are the same basic structures introduced on pp. 36–37, and will convey your desires clearly and easily. Before beginning to shop, however, you may first have to find the right store.

Excuse me, is there an antiques store around here?
Sumimasen, kono chikaku ni kottoya wa arimasuka?
すみません、この近くに骨董屋はありますか？

antique store	*kottoya*	骨董屋
bakery	*panya*	パン屋
barber shop	*tokoya*	床屋
beauty parlor	*biyōin*	美容院
bookstore	*honya*	本屋
camera shop	*kameraya*	カメラ屋
department store	*depāto*	デパート
drugstore	*yakkyoku*	薬局
electronics store	*denkiya*	電気屋
florist	*hanaya*	花屋
grocery store	*shokuryōhinten*	食料品店
hardware store	*kanamonoya*	金物屋
jewelry store	*hōsekiten*	宝石店
record store	*rekōdoten*	レコード店
shoe store	*kutsuya*	くつ屋
stationery store	*bunbōguya*	文房具店
supermarket	*sūpāmāketto*	スーパーマーケット
video rental store	*rentaru bideoya*	レンタルビデオ屋

The following expressions may be used when shopping for most anything. For specific types of goods, see the sections that follow. Naturally, you will also need to refer to NUMBERS and MONEY, pp. 18–21.

Is there a department store near here? (STORES, p. 137)
Kono chikaku ni depāto wa arimasuka?
この近くにデパートはありますか？

Where is [STORE NAME]?
[STORE NAME] wa doko desuka?
[店名]はどこですか？

Do you sell [ITEM]?
[ITEM] wa arimasuka?
[品名]はありますか？

I'd like to see this.
Kore *o misete kudasai.*
これを見せてください。

that	*sore*	それ
these	*korera*	これら
those	*sorera*	それら

Do you have any others?
Hoka ni arimasuka?
ほかにありますか？

Do you have a smaller one?   (ADJECTIVES, p. 84)
Motto chiisai *no wa arimasuka?*
もっと小さいのはありますか？

larger	*motto okii no*	もっと大きいの
cheaper	*motto yasui no*	もっと安いの
better	*motto yoi mono*	もっと良いもの

The Japanese yen floats against other major world currencies, so the exchange rate will vary from day to day. However, calculating 100 yen to one dollar will give you a ballpark price in U.S. currency.

Which do you recommend?
Dochira ga ii?
どちらがいい？

How much is it?
Ikura desuka?
いくらですか？

Please write down the price.
Nedan o kaite kudasai.
値段を書いてください。

Could you ship it for me?
Okutte kuremasuka?
送ってくれますか？

How much would it cost to ship?
Sōryō wa ikura desuka?
送料はいくらですか？

Do you accept credit cards?
Kurejitto kādo o tsukaemasuka?
ク.レジット・カードを使えますか？
U.S. dollars   *Amerika doru*   アメリカ・ドル
travelers' checks   *toraberāzu chekku*
　　　　　　　　　　トラベラーズ・チェック

May I have a receipt?
Reshiito o moraemasuka?
レシートをもらえますか？

Although the days of Oriental antiques going for a song are long past, there are still bargains for those willing to spend some time looking. In addition to antique stores, there are regularly scheduled flea markets (more properly "shrine fairs") held in and around Tokyo. Call one of the tourist organizations listed on p. 194 or consult a good up-to-date guidebook for detailed listings.

What's this?
Kore wa nan desuka?
これは何ですか？

What's it used for?
Nani ni tsukau no desuka?
何に使うのですか？

Do you have any traditional chests?
Tansu wa arimasuka?
タンスはありますか？

dolls	*ningyō*	人形
swords	*katana*	刀
pottery	*tōki*	陶器
ceramics	*setomono*	せともの
old coins	*kosen*	古銭
lacquerware	*shikki*	漆器
masks	*men*	面
helmets	*kabuto*	かぶと
kimono	*kimono*	きもの
kimono sashes	*obi*	帯
hanging scrolls	*kakemono*	掛物
ink paintings	*sumi-e*	墨絵
woodblock prints	*ukiyo-e*	浮世絵

The categories of arts, crafts, and antiques are mixed here because the Japanese traditionally did not distinguish between crafts and fine arts, and what were once craft items (furniture and prints, for example) are now often considered (and priced) as antique art objects. Moreover, in a land of earthquakes and fires, objects fashioned of wood and paper may obtain the status of antiques earlier than they might elsewhere.

Is this a replica?
Kore wa fukuseihin desuka?
これは複製品ですか？

How old is it?
Dore kurai mae no desuka?
どれくらい前のですか？

Do you have any bamboo umbrellas?
Bangasa wa arimasuka?
番傘はありますか？

bamboo blinds	*sudare*	すだれ
calligraphy brushes	*fude*	筆
chopstick rests	*hashioki*	箸置
drums	*taiko*	太鼓
folding fans	*sensu*	扇子
round fans	*uchiwa*	うちわ
wrapping cloths	*furoshiki*	風呂敷
shop curtains	*noren*	のれん
handmade paper	*washi*	和紙
patterned paper	*chiyogami*	千代紙
wooden dolls	*kokeshi*	こけし
wooden clogs	*geta*	げた
paper lanterns	*chōchin*	ちょうちん

Akihabara, the best place to browse for these items, is also one place in Japan you can bargain; if you don't like the price, a dozen shops on the same street carry the same item. Be sure to ask about the power requirements for plug-in items. Several stores, such as the LAOX group, have separate floors devoted to export models, staffed with English-speaking salespeople.

I'd like to buy a personal portable stereo.
Konpakuto sutereo setto o kudasai.
コンパクトステレオセットをください。

rack stereo system	*ōdio setto*	オーディオ・セット
cassette player	*kasetto pureiyā*	カセット・プレイヤー
receiver	*reshiibā*	レシーバー
tuner	*chūnā*	チューナー
headphones	*heddohon*	ヘッドフォン
speakers	*supiikā*	スピーカー
CD player	*CD purēyā*	CDプレーヤー
video deck	*bideo dekki*	ビデオ・デッキ
video camera	*bideo kamera*	ビデオ・カメラ
color TV	*karā terebi*	カラーテレビ

Can this be used in [COUNTRY]?
Kore wa [COUNTRY] de tsukaemasuka?
これは[国名]で使えますか？

Does it have an instruction manual in English?
Eigo no setsumeisho wa arimasuka?
英語の説明書はありますか？

Can you make it a little cheaper?
Sukoshi makete moraemasuka?
少しまけてもらえますか？

Shop at one of the discount stores in Shinjuku or Akihabara and show your passport to avoid sales tax (at authorized shops). Be sure to press for "a little better price," and compare prices between stores. For film processing and other photographic services, see p. 178.

Do you have a 35-mm camera?
***Sanjū-go miri kamera** wa arimasuka?*
35mmカメラはありますか?

automatic camera	*ōtomatikku kamera*	
	オートマチック・カメラ	
SLR camera	*ichiganrefu kamera*	
	一眼レフカメラ	
disposable camera	*tsukaisute kamera*	
	使い捨てカメラ	
zoom lens	*zūmu renzu*	ズーム・レンズ
wide-angle lens	*waido renzu*	ワイド・レンズ
telephoto lens	*bōen renzu*	望遠レンズ
battery	*batterii*	バッテリー
carrying case	*kyaringu kēsu*	キャリング・ケース
light meter	*raito mētā*	ライト・メーター
tripod	*sankyaku*	三脚

I need some color print film.
***Karā fuirumu** o kudasai.*
カラーフィルムをください。

color slide	*karā suraido*	カラー・スライド
black-and-white	*shirokuro*	白黒フィルム

Twenty-four exposures, please.   (COUNTERS, p. 23)
***Nijūyon maidori** no o kudasai.*
24枚どりのをください。

36 exposures	*sanjūroku maidori*	36枚どり
100 asa	*āsā hyaku*	アーサー100
400 asa	*āsā yonbyaku*	アーサー400

As with audio and video equipment, check power requirements or shop at special stores, or special floors in the stores, that feature export models.

I'd like to buy a rice cooker.
Suihanki o kudasai.
炊飯器をください。

coffee maker	*kōhii mēkā*	コーヒー・メーカー
fan	*senpūki*	扇風機
heater	*hiitā*	ヒーター
shaver	*sheibā*	シェイバー
steam iron	*suchiimu airon*	スチーム・アイロン
toaster oven	*ōbun tōsutā*	オーブン・トースター
microwave oven	*denshi renji*	電子レンジ
air conditioner	*eakon*	エアコン
bread maker	*panyakiki*	パン焼き機
humidifier	*kashitsuki*	加湿機
desk lamp	*takujō ranpu*	卓上ランプ
desk calculator	*dentaku*	電卓
alarm clock	*mezamashi dokei*	
	目覚まし時計	
clock radio	*tokei tsuki rajio*	
	時計付きラジオ	

Can this be used in [COUNTRY]?
Kore wa [COUNTRY] de tsukaemasuka?
これは[国名]で使えますか？

Does it have an instruction manual in English?
Eigo no setsumeisho wa arimasuka?
英語の説明書はありますか？

Can you make it a little cheaper?
Sukoshi makete moraemasuka?
少しまけてもらえますか？

The traditional Japanese hardware store, or *kana-monoya*, has items of interest for the tourist shopper as well as those planning a longer stay in Japan. Japanese saws, chisels, and woodworking tools are of world-renown quality, as are kitchen knives and cleavers, pruning shears, and other garden tools.

I want to buy a saw.
Nokogiri o kudasai.
のこぎりをください。

plane	*kanna*	カンナ
nails	*kugi*	くぎ
screws	*neji*	ねじ
pliers	*yattoko*	やっとこ
hammer	*kanazuchi*	金づち
file	*yasuri*	やすり
chisel	*nomi*	のみ
pruning shears	*edakiri basami*	枝切りバサミ
toolbox	*kōgubako*	工具箱
stepladder	*hashigo*	はしご
paint	*penki*	ペンキ
paintbrush	*hake*	ハケ
slot screwdriver	*mainasu no neji mawashi*	
	−のねじ回し	
Phillips screwdriver	*purasu no neji mawashi*	
	＋のねじ回し	

What's this?
Kore wa nan desuka?
これは何ですか？

What's it used for?
Nani ni tsukau no desuka?
何に使うのですか？

In addition to the Kanda-area stores mentioned earlier, English-language books are available at Kinokuniya (main store near Shinjuku Station), Maruzen (main store in Ginza), and at airport kiosks and hotel bookstores. English-language daily newspapers are also available at those locations, as well as at the kiosks of most major train stations.

Do you sell books in English?
Eigo no hon wa arimasuka?
英語の本はありますか？

Do you sell English-language newspapers?
Eiji shinbun wa arimasuka?
英字新聞はありますか？

Do you have [TITLE]?
[TITLE] no hon wa arimasuka?
[題名]の本はありますか？

Where can I find books on history?   (SUBJECTS p. 77)
Rekishi no hon wa doko desuka?
歴史の本はどこですか？

art	*bijutsu*	美術
economics	*keizai*	経済
Japan	*Nihon*	日本

Do you have guidebooks?
Gaidobukku wa arimasuka?
ガイドブックはありますか？

maps	*chizu*	地図
dictionaries	*jisho*	辞書
phrasebooks	*kanyōku jiten*	慣用句辞典
cookbooks	*ryōri no hon*	料理の本
detective novels	*suiri shōsetsu*	推理小説
fiction	*fikushon*	フィクション
poetry	*shi*	詩

Stationery departments and stores are great places to shop for small gifts to take back home, as Japanese design in writing utensils and desktop items is excellent. In addition, designs often incorporate a zany Japanese version of English, which Japanese regard as fashionable, and native English speakers often find amusing.

Where is the stationery department?
Bunbōguya wa doko desuka?
文房具屋はどこですか？

I'd like to buy a felt-tip pen.
Majikkupen o kudasai.
マジックペンをください。

fountain pen	*mannenhitsu*	万年筆
eraser	*keshigomu*	消しゴム
diary	*daiarii*	ダイアリー
address book	*adoresu bukku*	アドレス・ブック
appointment book	*yoteihyō*	予定表
photo album	*arubamu*	アルバム
stapler	*hotchikisu*	ホッチキス
notebook	*nōto*	ノート
envelope	*fūtō*	封筒
letter pad	*binsen*	便箋
scissors	*hasami*	ハサミ
razor knife	*kattā*	カッター
memo pad	*memochō*	メモ帳
cellophane tape	*serohan tēpu*	
	セロハン・テープ	
wrapping paper	*rappingu pēpā*	
	ラッピング・ペーパー	
gift writing set	*pen to shāpu pen no setto*	
	ペンとシャープペンのセット	

Shop for these in department stores or specialty shops, including franchised outlets of Western chains, such as Tower Records. Note that many analogue audio buffs collect Japanese phonograph records because of the supposedly high quality of the pressings. Album covers will have Japanese text, but liner notes are usually bilingual.

Where can I find jazz?
Jyazu wa doko desuka?
ジャズはどこですか？

classical music	*kurasikku*	クラシック
big band music	*biggu bando*	ビッグ・バンド
blues	*burūsu*	ブルース
rap music	*rappu*	ラップ
rock 'n' roll	*rokku*	ロック
golden oldies	*ōrudiizu*	オールディーズ
movie soundtracks	*eiga ongaku*	映画音楽
country and western	*kantori ando uestan*	
		カントリーアンドウェスタン
traditional music	*yōkyoku*	謡曲
Japanese pop music	*kayōkyoku*	歌謡曲
Japanese regional songs	*minyo*	民謡
Japanese contemporary ballads	*enka*	演歌

Does this come in a CD?
Kono CD arimasuka?
このCDありますか？

record	*rekōdo*	レコード
casette tape	*kasetto tēpu*	カセット・テープ

Note that Japanese clothes will be cut differently from their Western equivalents; a dress shirt with the correct neck size and sleeve length may be too tight in the chest, for example, and this may apply even to clothes with familiar labels, such as Brooks Brothers, which are licensed for local manufacture. If fit is important, therefore, it is wise to buy only what you can try on or what is tailor made.

Do you have dress shirts?
Waishatsu *wa arimasuka?*
ワイシャツはありますか？

sport shirt	*supōtsu shatsu*	スポーツ・シャツ
necktie	*nekutai*	ネクタイ
suit	*sūtsu*	スーツ
sport coat	*supōtsu kōto*	スポーツ・コート
belt	*beruto*	ベルト
pants	*zubon*	ズボン
shoes	*kutsu*	靴
socks	*kutsushita*	靴下
undershirts	*shitagi*	下着
boxer shorts	*bokusā shōtsu*	ボクサー・ショーツ
briefs	*buriifu*	ブリーフ
jacket	*jaketto*	ジャケット
overcoat	*kōto*	コート

Do you have a larger one?   (ADJECTIVES, p. 84)
Motto ookii no *arimasuka?*
もっと大きいのありますか？

smaller	*motto chiisai*	もっと小さいの
cheaper	*motto yasui*	もっと安いの
better	*motto yoi*	もっと良い
darker	*motto koi iro*	もっと濃い色
lighter	*motto akarui*	もっと明るい

Clothes bearing the labels of Japan's best boutiques have become as sought after as their haute couture counterparts in Paris and New York. For department store shopping, however, the advice given under "Men's Clothing" may apply as well.

Do you have dresses?
Fuku wa arimasuka?
服はありますか？

skirt	*sukāto*	スカート
slacks	*surakkusu*	スラックス
blouse	*burausu*	ブラウス
pantsuit	*pantsu sūtsu*	パンツ・スーツ
bra	*burajā*	ブラジャー
panties	*panti*	パンティー
pantyhose	*pansuto*	パンスト
shoes	*kutsu*	靴
stockings	*sutokkingu*	ストッキング
swimsuit	*mizugi*	水着

Do you have it in green?
Guriin wa arimasuka?
グリーンはありますか？

brown	*chairo*	茶色
red	*aka*	赤
black	*kuro*	黒
white	*shiro*	白
orange	*orenji*	オレンジ
blue	*ao*	青
yellow	*kiiro*	黄色

COSMETICS AND JEWELRY 151

Japanese cosmetic makers have not attained the worldwide status enjoyed by the best Western houses, although their products are of good quality and highly valued and sought after by the women of Asia. And Japan is definitely not the place to buy fine jewelry, although the basic vocabulary is included here in case of a "social emergency."

Do you have cosmetics.
Keshōhin wa arimasuka?
化粧品はありますか？

perfume	*kōsui*	香水
compact	*konpakuto*	コンパクト
pressed powder	*paudā*	パウダー
foundation	*fandēshon*	ファンデーション
blusher	*hōbeni*	ほお紅
eyebrow pencil	*aiburō penshiru*	アイブロー・ペンシル
eye liner	*airainā*	アイライナー
eye shadow	*aishadō*	アイシャドー
mascara	*masukara*	マスカラ
lipstick	*kuchibeni*	口紅
clarifying lotion	*keshōsui*	化粧水
nail polish	*neiru porisshu*	ネイル・ポリッシュ
polish remover	*rimūbā*	リムーバー
jewelry	*hōseki*	宝石
necklace	*nekkuresu*	ネックレス
bracelet	*buresuretto*	ブレスレット
broach	*burōchi*	ブローチ

Japan produces little domestic leather, so shoes tend to be expensive, and fashion-conscious Japanese of means choose imported brands or foreign brands manufactured under license. Leather goods and luggage, likewise, will be expensive. Japanese brands of sports shoes are excellent, although most are actually manufactured elsewhere in Asia.

Do you have tennis shoes?
Tenisu shūzu wa arimasuka?
テニス・シューズはありますか？。

jogging shoes	*jogingu shūzu*	ジョギング・シューズ
dress shoes	*doresu shūzu*	ドレス・シューズ
casual shoes	*kajuaru shūzu*	カジュアル・シューズ
loafers	*rōfā*	ローファー
flats	*furatto*	フラット
boots	*būtsu*	ブーツ
shoe polish	*kutsu migaki*	靴みがき
shoe brush	*burashi*	ブラシ
suitcase	*sūtsukēsu*	スーツケース
garment bag	*ishō baggu*	衣装バッグ
overnight bag	*ryokō kaban*	旅行カバン
cosmetic case	*keshōbako*	化粧箱
briefcase	*buriifukēsu*	ブリーフケース
portfolio	*orikaban*	折りカバン

These are a bit small.   (ADJECTIVES, p. 84)
Sukoshi chiisai desu.
少し小さいです。

big	*ōkii*	大きい
expensive	*takai*	高い
heavy	*omoi*	重い
flimsy	*usupperai*	うすっぺらい

This is one of few categories of consumer goods for which Japanese tend to prefer foreign brands — the per capita possession of Hermes and Louis Vuitton products is staggering. Japanese watches, which no well-dressed Japanese would be without, are an exception, being of the highest quality and available in every price range.

Do you have a wristwatch?
Udedokei wa arimasuka?
腕時計はありますか？

gloves	*tebukuro*	手袋
umbrella	*kasa*	傘
folding umbrella	*oritatamigasa*	折りたたみ傘
parasol	*higasa*	日傘
hat	*bōshi*	帽子
earmuffs	*mimiate*	耳あて
scarf	*sukāfu*	スカーフ
wallet	*saifu*	さいふ
purse	*pāsu*	パース
coin purse	*kozeniire*	小銭入
belt	*beruto*	ベルト
suspenders	*sasupendā*	サスペンダー
pocket watch	*poketto uotchi*	ポケット・ウォッチ

Do you have a less expensive one? (ADJECTIVES, p. 84)
Motto yasui no wa arimasuka?
もっと安いのはありますか？

Do you have one made in Japan?
Nihonsei no wa arimasuka?
日本製のはありますか？

Do you have another color?
Hoka no iro mo arimasuka?
他の色もありますか？

Japanese are avid participants in all sports, and Japanese-made equipment for many of these has become widely recognized as of the highest quality. Golf clubs, fishing gear, bicycles, and ski equipment are particularly well designed and well made.

Do you have fishing gear?
Tsurigu wa arimasuka?
つり具はありますか？

fishing rod	*tsurizao*	釣り竿
fishing reel	*riiru*	リール
hook	*tsuribari*	釣針
float	*uki*	うき
lure	*gijie*	疑似餌
sinker	*omori*	おもり
fishing line	*tsuri ito*	釣糸
swimsuit	*mizugi*	水着
goggles	*gōguru*	ゴーグル
diver's mask	*suichu megane*	水中メガネ
fins	*fin*	フィン
snorkel	*shunōkeru*	シュノーケル
scuba gear	*sukyūbā yōgu*	スキューバー用具
skiwear	*sukii uea*	スキー・ウエア
ski poles	*sutokku*	ストック
skis	*sukii ita*	スキー板
ski boots	*sukii būtsu*	スキー・ブーツ
ski bindings	*tomegane*	止め金

Do not expect to find a bargain on fishing gear if you are in Japan in winter, or a spring skiwear sale; due to the inventory constraints imposed by scarcity of space, goods for the sports of the season are usually all that are on display.

Do you have camping gear?
***Kyanpudogu** wa arimasuka?*
キャンプ道具はありますか？

camp stove	*kyanpu sutōbu*	キャンプ・ストーブ
lantern	*ranpu*	ランプ
backpack	*bakkupakku*	バックパック
hiking shoes	*haikingu shūzu*	ハイキング・シューズ
canteen	*suitō*	水筒
cook kit	*suihan yogu*	炊飯用具
tent	*tento*	テント
sleeping bag	*nebukuro*	寝袋
basketball	*basuketto bōru*	バスケット・ボール
football	*futto bōru*	フット・ボール
soccer ball	*sakkā bōru*	サッカー・ボール
baseball	*yakyū*	野球
baseball bat	*batto*	バット
baseball glove	*gurōbu*	グローブ
golf balls	*gorufu bōru*	ゴルフ・ボール
golf bags	*gorufu baggu*	ゴルフ・バッグ
golf clubs	*gorufu kurabu*	ゴルフ・クラブ
weights	*ueito*	ウェイト
jump rope	*nawatobinawa*	なわとび縄

Japan's food markets are a joy to browse, for as with Japanese cuisine, freshness, seasonality, and presentation are emphasized. Even for the tourist uninterested in grocery bargains, shops and supermarkets offer a glimpse into the everyday life of ordinary Japanese. Chicken and pork are reasonably priced in Japan; good beef is quite expensive.

Do you have pork chops?
Pōku choppu wa arimasuka?
ポークチョップはありますか？

bacon	*bēkon*	ベーコン
beef	*biifu*	ビーフ
hamburger	*hikiniku*	挽肉
sirloin steak	*sāroin sutēki*	サーロイン・ステーキ
chicken	*tori*	鳥
chicken wings	*tebasaki*	手羽先
chicken thighs	*torimomo*	鳥もも
chicken breasts	*muneniku*	胸肉
liver	*rebā*	レバー
spare ribs	*supea ribu*	スペアリブ
pork	*pōku*	ポーク
roast pork	*rōsuto pōku*	ロースト・ポーク

I need one hundred grams, please.   (NUMBERS, p. 21)
Hyaku guramu o kudasai.
百グラムをください。

five hundred grams	*go hyaku guramu*	五百グラム
one kilo	*ichi kiro*	一キロ

Outside of specialty fish markets, there are few retail outlets in the U.S. whose seafood offerings rival those of an ordinary Japanese supermarket. Since this is a country where seafood is routinely served raw, as sushi and sashimi, freshness is accorded the highest importance.

Do you have abalone?
Awabi wa arimasuka?
あわびはありますか？

Atka mackerel	*hokke*	ほっけ
bonito	*katsuo*	鰹
clam	*hamaguri*	はまぐり
cod	*tara*	鱈
crab	*kani*	蟹
eel	*unagi*	うなぎ
flounder	*hirame*	平目
herring	*nishin*	鯡
horse mackerel	*aji*	鯵
octopus	*tako*	タコ
oyster	*kaki*	牡蛎
salmon	*sake*	鮭
sardine	*iwashi*	鰯
trout	*masu*	鱒
Pacific saury	*sanma*	秋刀魚
scallop	*hotategai*	帆立貝
short-necked clam	*asari*	浅蜊
shrimp	*ebi*	海老
squid	*ika*	イカ
tuna	*maguro*	鮪
yellowtail	*buri*	鰤

Typically grown on tiny plots of valuable land by farmers employing little mechanized assistance, Japanese vegetables are relatively expensive. However, what is in season is often a bargain.

Do you have asparagus?
Asupara (gasu) wa arimasuka?
アスパラ（ガス）はありますか？

broccoli	*burokkorii*	ブロッコリー
cabbage	*kyabetsu*	キャベツ
spinach	*hōrensō*	ほうれん草
bell pepper	*piiman*	ピーマン
green bean	*guriin piisu*	グリーンピース
sweet potato	*satsuma imo*	さつま芋
squash	*kabocha*	かぼちゃ
carrot	*ninjin*	人参
radish	*daikon*	大根
turnip	*kabu*	かぶ
bean sprout	*moyashi*	もやし
brussel sprout	*mekyabetsu*	芽キャベツ
cucumber	*kyūri*	キュウリ
leaf lettuce	*retasu*	レタス
eggplant	*nasu*	茄子
green onion	*negi*	ネギ
yellow onion	*tamanegi*	タマネギ
bamboo shoot	*takenoko*	竹の子

Fruits are also expensive, both for the reasons given for vegetables and because many are imported. It is true that you can actually pay $200 for a single melon.

Do you have apples?
Ringo wa arimasuka?
リンゴはありますか？

apricot	*apurikotto*	アプリコット
peach	*momo*	桃
raisin	*hoshibudō*	干しぶどう
banana	*banana*	バナナ
watermelon	*suika*	西瓜
tangerine	*mikan*	蜜柑
pear	*nashi*	梨
persimmon	*kaki*	柿
lemon	*remon*	レモン

Are these ready to eat?
Kore wa tabegoro desuka?
これは食べ頃ですか？

How much are these apiece?
Kore wa ikko ikura desuka?
これは一個いくらですか？

How much are these per kilo?
Kore wa ichikiro ikura desuka?
これは1キロいくらですか？

Japanese sell Western-style baked goods both in super-markets and bakeries. Although these can be quite good, some items (curry doughnuts, for example) will surely surprise Western taste buds.

Do you have rye bread?
Raimugi pan wa arimasuka?
ライ麦パンはありますか？

white bread	*shoku pan*	食パン
whole wheat bread	*genmai pan*	玄米パン
French bread	*furansu pan*	フランスパン
doughnut	*dōnattsu*	ドーナッツ
pastry	*kashi pan*	菓子パン
bagel	*bēguru*	ベーグル
cookies	*kukkii*	クッキー
cake	*kēki*	ケーキ
pie	*pai*	パイ
potato chips	*poteto chippusu*	ポテトチップス
popcorn	*poppukōn*	ポップコーン
cereal	*shiriaru*	シリアル
pasta	*pasuta*	パスタ
croissant	*kurowassan*	クロワッサン
sweet bean bun	*anpan*	アンパン
custard cream bun	*kuriim pan*	クリームパン
tart	*taruto*	タルト
rice cracker	*okaki*	おかき

A long stay in Japan can be made easier and more economical if you learn to cook a few Japanese dishes.
Essential ingredients are soy, sake (rice wine), and a
soup stock called *dashi*, made with *konbu* (kelp),
dried sardines, and bonito flakes. However, ask for
dashinomoto at the market and you will get a pow-
dered, instant variety that makes a perfectly acceptable
and convenient substitute.

Do you have pickled plums?
***Umeboshi** wa arimasuka?*
梅ぼしはありますか？

dried seaweed	*nori*	のり
pickled vegetables	*oshinko*	おしんこ
dried bonito	*katsuobushi*	かつお節
dried kelp	*kobu*	コブ
burdock root	*gobō*	ごぼう
devil's tongue	*konnyaku*	こんにゃく
buckwheat noodles	*soba*	ソバ
wheat-flour noodles	*udon*	ウドン
Japanese horseradish	*wasabi*	わさび
cod roe	*tarako*	たらこ
Japanese soup base	*dashinomoto*	だしの素
instant noodles	*sokuseki rāmen*	
	即席ラーメン	
instant miso soup	*sokuseki misoshiru*	
	即席味噌汁	

Shopping for drinks is usually no problem for the foreigner in Japan, because everything (except dairy products) from small cans of soda to liters of whiskey is sold from vending machines. These are located in front of mom-and-pop convenience stores found in every residential neighborhood.

Do you have tomato juice?
Tomato jūsu wa arimasuka?
トマトジュースはありますか？

orange juice	*orenji jūsu*	オレンジ・ジュース
cola	*kōra*	コーラ
milk	*miruku*	ミルク
skim milk	*sukimu miruku*	スキムミルク
beer	*biiru*	ビール
draft beer	*nama biiru*	生ビール
beer in bottles	*bin iri biiru*	ビン入りビール
beer in cans	*kan biiru*	缶ビール
scotch	*sukotchi*	スコッチ
bourbon	*bābon*	バーボン
gin	*jin*	ジン
vodka	*uokka*	ウォッカ
tonic water	*tonikku uōtā*	トニックウォーター
seltzer water	*serutsā*	セルツァー
club soda	*kurabu sōda*	クラブソーダ
sake	*Nihonshu*	日本酒
shochu	*shōchū*	ショーチュウ
red wine	*aka wain*	赤ワイン
white wine	*shiro wain*	白ワイン
rose	*rose*	ロゼ

In service-oriented Japan, simply asking a clerk whether the store carries a particular item is usually sufficient to compel him or her to help you find it. If not, the last question below should make your need explicit.

Do you have salad oil?
Saradayu wa arimasuka?
サラダ油はありますか？

salt	*shio*	塩
pepper	*koshō*	胡椒
garlic	*ninniku*	にんにく
ginger	*shōga*	生姜
flour	*komugiko*	小麦粉
soy sauce	*shōyu*	醤油
sesame oil	*goma abura*	ゴマ油
corn starch	*kōn sutāchi*	コーンスターチ
bullion cubes	*kokei sūpu*	固形スープ

Do you have a larger size?
Motto ōkii no wa arimasuka?
もっと大きいのはありますか？

Do you have a smaller size?
Motto chiisai no wa arimasuka?
もっと小さいのはありますか？

Where is it?
Doko desuka?
どこですか？

A Day in the Life of a Depāto

For the visitor with little time to seek out specialty shops or to wander the particular areas of the city mentioned earlier, Japan's ubiquitous department stores offer the best overview of the country's shopping possibilities. More than this, however, a half day or so spent at a department store probably offers the quickest and best introduction to modern Japan one can get.

• Pick a large store for your visit, one at a main station or in a major shopping area. Try the Mitsukoshi or Takashimaya in Ginza if you want to see where more conservative, monied Japan shops; visit the massive Seibu in Shibuya if you want to see what appeals to the affluent young. And go early, not so much to avoid crowds as to enjoy a small taste of Japanese service — the lines of bowing salespeople welcoming the first customers of the day.

• Pick up a floor guide (generally available in English) at the information counter and head out toward what interests you. In addition to familiar-looking departments featuring goods available in the West, these stores offer a full range of traditional items. Besides boutique areas featuring the latest designer fashions, for example, there will be an area devoted to traditional Japanese clothing, usually with a shop that custom tailors kimono from the beautiful fabrics displayed. These, of course, will be quite costly, but in the same area you can probably pick up an inexpensive summer-weight cotton robe called a *yukata* that makes an elegant and useful souvenir.

• West and East, or modern and traditional, are paralled in other departments such as kitchenware, where you will find modern cooking dishes and utensils adjacent to, or nearby, sushi knives, bamboo rice steamers, and chopstick rests. There is usually a sizeable area devoted to finely crafted objects for home use and decoration, including lacquerware, carved woodenware, and pottery. Prices here range from moderate to those that would be expected for objects hand-crafted and signed by noted artisans.

• Besides seeking out items to purchase for yourself, it is fun to see what the Japanese are buying. The toy, book and magazine, musical instrument, and sporting goods departments will all display goods that are not available in your neighborhood Sears back home, and they are good places to find small gifts to take back that are both representative of Japan and likely not available in tourist gift shops.

• At some point Japan's department stores seem to have decided that taking on the social role of purveyors of culture for the masses was good for business. Most of the larger stores, therefore, have art museums, usually located on one of the upper floors. Although these are typically small, they often mount impressive exhibits, and the diffusion of department stores throughout the metropolitan area means that there is usually an interesting exhibit to be seen somewhere nearby.

• Japan's department store designers also wisely decided at some point that it was bad business to let shoppers escape just because they wanted something particular to eat. So most stores have not one, but a whole floor of restaurants, offering a wide range of both Japanese and Western (Japanized Western, actually) dishes. In the interests of keeping shoppers contented, prices are low; for budget-conscious travelers, a department store lunch is sensible idea.

• On the subject of food, one shouldn't miss the underground supermarkets, in some larger stores occupying two basement floors. To maintain the small-shop ambience that Japanese housewives favor, foods are often grouped in separate islands, each staffed by what appears an inordinate number of salespeople yelling out their specials and liberally dispensing free samples. Truly budget-conscious travelers might want to spend some time here.

• And don't forget the roof. Remember, space is at a premium in Japan and savvy merchants do not let this valuable area go to waste. Some big department stores use the roof for gardening and greenery shops, so that plants show off well and can be easily tended. Other stores include their pet departments, featuring fish and birds, to enhance the "wild outdoors" effect. Children's amusements — games and rides — are also often installed here, so parents can park their offspring while they shop.

• In the summertime, the spacious rooftops of some department stores (Seibu in Shibuya and

Takashimaya in Ginza, for example) become beer gardens. Although "garden" is stretching the term when they are compared with their German antecedents, still, festive lanterns and the possibility of cool evening breezes make them pleasant places to enjoy good Japanese beer and a light snack after shopping. Although department stores hours are typically ten to seven, the beer gardens usually stay open much later, and are accessible by separate elevators and entrances.

• Unlike their counterparts in the West, typically situated in distant malls, Japanese department stores are always conveniently located at public transportation hubs. In fact, several of the larger transportation companies, including Seibu, Hankyu, Odakyu, and Keio, are affiliated with department store chains, so that it appears the primary aim of their routes is to deliver their customers directly to their stores.

• To get around easily on your department store tour, the following expressions may be useful:

What floor is [DEPARTMENT] on?
[DEPARTMENT] wa nankai desuka?
［売場］は何階ですか？

Where is the elevator?
Erebētā wa doko desuka?
エレベーターはですか？

Is there a service center for foreign customers?
Gaikokujin-kyaku sābisu sentā wa arimasuka?
外国人客サービスセンターはありますか？

Getting It Done

Unlike the purchase of goods, obtaining services may require higher-level language skills than a simple phrasebook can provide. However, the words and expressions listed here should get you started, after which the innate politeness and "host complex" of the Japanese should work to ensure that you ultimately get what you need. In this chapter you will also find information and language useful for handling any emergencies that might arise.

Medical and Other Emergencies

With the highest possible sanitary standards, Japan poses no health risks for the foreign visitor, and no inoculations or precautionary measures are needed before traveling there. Unlike elsewhere in Asia, water in Japan is safe to drink from the tap, and the traditional diet has contributed toward making the Japanese among the world's longest lived people. A high regard for social values and harmony, as well more practical factors like an efficent and disciplined police force and laws restricting the private ownership of guns, have made violent crime rare; it is safe to walk the streets at night anywhere in the country.

hospital 病院 *byōin*
Major cities have hospitals with English-speaking staff and doctors *(issha)* who speak English (see p. 197). The clinics of major tourist hotels often have English-speaking physicians on staff, and even if they do not, a

tourist hotel is a good place to begin your search for medical help, due to the presence of English-speaking Japanese to assist you.

pharmacy 薬屋 *kusuriya* （薬局 *yakkyoku*）
Japanese pharmacies sell over-the-counter and prescription drugs manufactured both in Japan and in the West. To avoid problems, bring a supply of prescription drugs generous enough to see you through your stay in Japan.

police box 交番 *kōban*
One reason often cited for Japan's low crime rate is the presence of the "beat cop," sometimes referred to as *omawarisan* (literally "Mr. Go Around"). These police patrol the streets, usually on bicycles, and can be contacted at the *kōban*, the small "police box" located in each neighborhood. You can also dial 110 to call the police, or 119 to report a fire.

Help! 助けて *Tasukete!*
The urgency of this imperative form of the verb "to help" is shown by the fact that the normally polite ending *kudasai* is omitted. Screaming or yelling this should attract attention in an emergency (although a foreigner in Japan screaming anything will attract attention). Use the fuller expression *Chotto tasukete kudasai* ("Please help me a little") to get assistance for less urgent matters.

Beginning students of Japanese are invariably amused that the word for beauty parlor (pronounced *bi-YO-in*, with the stress on the middle syllable), is so similar to the word for hospital, *BYO-in* (with the stress on the first two syllables combined). If you are concerned that your quest for a beautician will lead you to the emergency ward, point to your head as you ask.

Where can I get my hair done?
Biyōin wa doko desuka?
美容院はどこですか？

Is there a beauty parlor nearby?
Kono chikaku ni biyōin wa arimasuka?
この近くに美容院はありますか？

I'd like a shampoo and set.
Shanpū to setto o onegaishimasu.
シャンプーとセットをお願いします。

permanent wave	*pāma*	パーマ
haircut	*hea katto*	ヘアカット
manicure	*manikyua*	マニキュア
pedicure	*pedikyua*	ペディキュア

I want it to look like this.
Konoyō ni shite kudasai.
この様にしてください。

How long will it take?
Dore gurai no jikan ga kakarimasuka?
どれぐらいの時間がかかりますか？

I want it to look like this.
Konoyō ni shite kudasai.
この様にしてください。

A visit to a Japanese barber shop, or *tokoya*, can be an introduction to the thoroughness of Japanese service. Most customers take this opportunity to get the full treatment: shampoo, haircut, shave (often included), mustache trim, manicure, neck massage, and even a short nap.

Is there a barber shop nearby?
Kono chikaku ni tokoya wa arimasuka?
この近くに床屋はありますか？

How long is the wait?
Dore gurai machimasuka?
どれぐらい待ちますか？

I'd like a haircut.
Hea katto o onegai shimasu.
ヘアカットをお願いします。

shave	*higesori*	ひげそり
trim	*soroeru*	そろえる
shampoo	*shanpū*	シャンプー
manicure	*manikyua*	マニキュア

I part my hair here.
Koko de wakemasu.
ここで分けます。

Take off a little more here.
Koko o mō sukoshi mijikaku shite kudasai.
ここをもう少し短くしてください。

It looks fine.
Kore de kekkō desu.
これでけっこうです。

Coin laundries are comparable in price to those in the West. The washing machines are quite small, however, and usually use cold water. Coin laundries are usually found at the neighborhood public bath, or *sento*, making these convenient one-stop cleaning centers.

Is there a coin laundry nearby?
Kono chikaku ni koin randorii wa arimasuka?
この近くにコインランドリーはありますか？

Is there laundry service here?
Koko ni randorii sābisu wa arimasuka?
ここにランドリー・サービスはありますか？

Is there a sento nearby?
Kono chikaku ni sento wa arimasuka?
この近くに銭湯はありますか？

I'd like these washed.
*Kore o **sentaku** shite kudasai.*
これを洗濯してください。

mended	*naoshi*	直し
ironed only	*airongake dake*	
	アイロンがけだけ	
washed and ironed	*sentaku to airongake*	
	洗濯とアイロンがけ	

Is the bath open?
Ofuro wa aite imasuka?
お風呂は開いていますか？

How much is it?
Ikura desuka?
いくらですか？

Hotel laundry services are typical of those elsehwere: good but expensive. You can save a bit by using the small dry cleaning shops and coin laundries located in most neighborhoods.

Is there a dry cleaner nearby?
Kono chikaku ni doraikuriininguya wa arimasuka?
この近くにドライ・クリーニング屋はありますか？

I want this dry cleaned.
*Kore o **doraikuriiningu** de onegai shimasu.*
これをドライ・クリーニングでお願いします。

mended	*naoshi*	直し
pressed only	*puresugake dake*	
	プレスがけだけ	
cleaned and pressed	*doraikuriiningu to puresu*	
	ドライ・クリーニングとプレス	

I'd like this stain taken out.
Kono shimi o totte hoshiino desuga.
このしみをとってほしいのですが。

No starch, please.
Nori nashi de onegaishimasu.
のりなしでお願いします。

| folded | *tatamu* | たたむ |
| on hangars | *hangā* | ハンガー |

When will they be ready?
Itsu dekimasuka?
いつ出来ますか？

I need them right away.
Sugu hitsuyō nano desuga.
すぐ必要なのですが。

Tailoring in Japan is excellent and, as one would expect, fairly expensive.

Can you recommend a good tailor?
Ii tērā o shittemasuka?
いいテーラーを知ってますか？

I'd like to have a shirt made. (CLOTHING, pp. 149–150)
Waishatu o tsukuritai no desuga.
ワイシャツをつくりたいのですが。

| dress | *doresu* | ドレス |
| suit | *sūtsu* | スーツ |

I'd like it made like this.
Konoyō ni tsukutte hoshii no desuga.
この様につくってほしいのですが。

I'd like these taken up.
*Suso o **agete** kudasai.*
裾を上げてください。

let out	*dasu*	出す
altered	*kaeru*	変える
mended	*naosu*	直す

When will it be ready?
Istu dekimasuka?
いつ出来ますか？

When should I come back?
Itsu tori ni kitara ii desuka?
いつ取りに来たらいいですか？

Shoeshine stands located outside of major train stations also do minor shoe repairs. In addition, there is a nationwide chain of "Mr. Minute" shoe repair kiosks, which will do the work while you wait.

Where can I get these polished?
Doko de kutsu o migakemasuka?
どこで靴をみがけますか？

I'd like my shoes polished.
Kutsu o migaite hoshii no desuga.
靴をみがいてほしいのですが。

Is there a shoe repair place around here?
Kono chikaku ni kutsu no shūriya wa arimasuka?
この近くに靴の修理屋はありますか？

Where can I get this fixed?
Doko de kore o naoshite kuremasuka?
どこでこれを直してくれますか？

I want this fixed.
Kore o naoshite kudasai.
これを直してください。

I want new soles.
Kutsuzoko o harikuete kudasai.
靴底をはり変えてください。

| heels | *kakato* | カカト |
| soles and heels | *kutsuzoko to kakato* | 靴底とカカト |

Can you do it while I wait?
Matte iru uchi ni dekimasuka?
待っている内に出来ますか？

The Japanese postal system is very efficient and post offices are open six days a week (until noon on Saturdays). If you must use English to make your mission understood, go to one of the main offices.

I want to pick up a package.
Nimotsu o uketoritai no desuga.
荷物を受け取りたいのですが。

I want to send a package.
Nimotsu o okuritai no desuga.
荷物を送りたいのですが。

I want to send a registered letter.
Kakitome o okuritai no desuga.
書留を送りたいのですが。

I want to buy some stamps.
***Kitte** o kudasai.*
切手をください。

postcards	*hagaki*	ハガキ
air letters	*kōkūshokan*	航空書簡
boxes	*hako*	箱

I'd like to buy ten ¥100 stamps.   (COUNTERS, p. 23)
Hyakuen kitte o jūmai kudasai.
100円切手を10枚ください。

I want to send this to the U.S.
Kore o Amerika ni okuritai no desuga.
これをアメリカに送りたいのですが。

I want to send this as "printed matter."
Kore o insatsubutsu de okuritai no desuga
これを印刷物で送りたいのですが。

Postage for an air letter to the U.S. or Canada is ¥100; ¥120 to Europe. Postcards are ¥70 to anywhere. Note that SAL, below, stands for "Surface Air Lifted," an international delivery system that is faster and costlier than sea mail, but cheaper and slower than air mail.

I want to send this by air mail.
Kore o eamēru de okuritai no desuga.
これをエア・メールで送りたいのですが。

| registered mail | *kakitome* | 書留 |
| SAL | *esu ei eru* | エス・エイ・エール |

I want to send this the cheapest way.
Kore o ichiban yasui no de okuritai no desuga.
これを一番安いので送りたいのですが。

| fastest way | *ichiban hayai* | 一番早い |
| safest way | *ichiban anzen na bōhō* | 一番安全な方法 |

I want to insure this for ¥10,000.   (MONEY, p. 24)
Kore ni ichimanen no hoken o kaketai no desuga.
これに1万円の保険をかけたいのですが。

Inside are books.
Nakami wa hon desu.
中身は本です。

| clothes | *fuku* | 服 |
| presents | *gifuto* | ギフト |

How much is the postage?
Ikura desuka?
いくらですか？

How long will it take to get there?
Nannichi gurai de tsukimasuka?
何日ぐらいで着きますか？

Japanese are avid photographers. Kiosks and small shops offering speedy development services can be found in major train and subway stations.

Where can I get film developed?
Doko de firumu no genzō ga dekimasuka?
どこでフィルムの現像が出来ますか？

I'd to get these developed.
Genzō o onegai shimasu.
現像お願いします。

I'd like glossy prints.
Gurosu shiage de onegai shimasu.
グロス仕上げでお願いします。

I'd like matte finish.
Matto shiage de onegai shimasu.
マット仕上げでお願いします。

How much is it per roll?
Ippon ikura desuka?
一本いくらですか？

When can I pick them up?
Itsu dekimasuka?
いつ出来ますか？

I'd like a copy of this one.
Kore o purinto shitai no desuga.
これをプリントしたいのですが。

Two prints each, please.   (COUNTERS, p. 23)
Nimai zutsu purinto shite kudasai.
2枚ずつプリントしてください。

Stationery stores as well as 24-hour convenience stores typically offer business services to neighborhood clients, who may send a fax when they pick up some bread and milk.

Where can I send a fax?
Doko de fakkusu o okuremasuka?
どこでファックスを送れますか？

Where can I get some copies made?
Doko de kopii o shite moraemasuka?
どこでコピーをしてもらえますか？

I'd like to send this by fax.
Fakkusu o okuritai no desuga.
ファックスを送りたいのですが。

Here's the number.
Kore ga bangō desu.
これが番号です。

Here's the country code.
Kore ga kantorii kōdo desu.
これがカントリー・コードです。

I'd like three copies of this.   (COUNTERS, p. 23)
Kore o sanmai kopii shite kudasai.
これを3枚コピーしてください。

I'd like to make this smaller.
Kore o shukushō shite kudasai.
これを縮小してください。

I like to get this blown up.
Kore o kakudai shite kudasai.
これを拡大してください。

In Japan, as in 1950s America, well-groomed, uniformed attendants still automatically check the oil and water, and clean the windows as your car is being fueled, while you read magazines in an air-conditioned waiting room.

Fill it up, please.
Mantan de onegai shimasu.
満タンでお願いします。

Are the oil and water OK?
Oiru to mizu wa daijōbu desuka?
オイルと水は大丈夫ですか？

I'd like to have the car washed.
Sensha o onegai shimasu.
洗車をお願いします。

There seems to be something wrong with the engine.
Enjin ga okashii yō desu.
エンジンがおかしい様です。

brakes	*burēki*	ブレーキ
transmission	*toransumisshon*	トランスミッション
steering	*handoru*	ハンドル
headlights	*heddoraito*	ヘッドライト
tail lights	*tēruranpu*	テールランプ
windshield wipers	*waipā*	ワイパー
heater	*hiitā*	ヒーター
air conditioner	*eakon*	エアコン
radio	*rajio*	ラジオ

Good service is usually provided by neighborhood shops *if* you purchased the product there. In Japan however, where new means clean and clean means beautiful, broken or defective items are quickly discarded. Budget-conscious foreign residents have been known to furnish entire apartments with items rescued from neighborhood trash and repaired.

This doesn't work.
Kore ga ugokimasen.
これが動きません。

I'd like to get this fixed.
Kore o naoshite kudasai.
これを直してください。

Can this be fixed?
Kore wa naorimasuka?
これは直りますか？

How much will it cost?
Ikura kakarimasuka?
いくらかかりますか？

How much will a new one cost?
Atarashii no wa ikura desuka?
新しいのはいくらですか？

How long will it take?
Nannichi gurai kakarimasuka?
何日ぐらいかかりますか？

Telephone numbers of travel services are listed on pp.
194–196. For budget travel outside Japan booked from
Japan, check listings in the *Japan Times* classified section.

Is there a JR Travel Service Center near here?
Kono chikaku ni JR no sābisu sentā wa arimasuka?
この近くにJRのサービスセンターはありますか？

Japan Travel Bureau office	*JTB no ofisu*
	JTBのオフィス
tourist information center	*kankō annaijō*
	観光案内所

Which way is it?
Doko desuka?
どこですか？

I'd to stay at a Japanese inn. (ACCOMMODATIONS, p. 40)
Ryokan ni tomaritai no desuga.
旅館に泊まりたいのですが。

visit this place	*koko ni ikitai*
	ここに行きたい
arrange for a home stay	*bōmu sutei o shitai*
	ホームスティをしたい
take a tour of the city	*shinaikankō o shitai*
	市内観光をしたい

Do you have a map of the area?
Soko no chizu wa arimasuka?
そこの地図はありますか？

English maps	*Eigo no chizu* 英語の地図
English brochures	*Eigo no panfuretto*
	英語のパンフレット

Tickets to major events — concerts, plays, games — can be booked through ticket agencies (p. 196), while traditional entertainments, such as kabuki and sumo, have box offices at their respective venues.

I want to go to this game.
*Kono **shiai** o mitai no desuga.*
この試合を観たいのですが。

concert	*konsāto*	コンサート
play	*shibai*	芝居
movie	*eiga*	映画

What time does it begin?   (TIME, p. 26)
Kaien wa nanji desuka?
開演は何時ですか？

I'd like to buy two tickets.   (COUNTERS, p. 23)
Nimai kudasai.
2枚ください。

How much are they apiece?   (MONEY, p. 24)
Ichimai ikura desuka?
一枚いくらですか？

Can you show me where the seats are?
Seki ga dokoka misete moraemasuka?
席がどこか見せてもらえますか？

Are there any other seats?
*Hoka no **seki** wa arimasuka?*
ほかの席はありますか？

| times | *jikan* | 時間 |
| days | *hinichi* | 日にち |

In Japan, the doctor is the unquestioned authority, and may not be as forthcoming or detailed about his diagnosis as his Western counterpart.

Is there a doctor who speaks English?
Eigo o hanasu isha wa imasuka?
英語を話す医者はいますか？

Does anyone speak English?
Dareka Eigo ga hanasemasuka?
誰か英語が話せますか？

It hurts here.
Koko ga itai no desuga.
ここが痛いのですが。

It hurts when I do this.
Kōsuru to itai desu.
こうすると痛いです。

I feel sick.
Kimochi warui desu.
気持ちわるいです。

have indigestion	*shōka furyō*	消化不良
am constipated	*benpi*	便秘
have diarrhea	*geri*	下痢

I have a fever.
Netsu ga arimasu.
熱があります。

| chest pains | *mune ni itami* | 胸に痛み |
| sore throat | *nodo ni itami* | のどに痛み |

I've had a heart attack.
Shinzōmahi ni narimashita.
心臓マヒになりました。

You should have no trouble locating an English-speaking physician if you have plenty of time. If you cannot, however, it is advisable to take along someone who can interpret for you, unless your symptoms are readily apparent.

I have a cold.
Kaze o hiita.
かぜをひいた。

I feel nauseous.
Hakike *ga shimasu.*
吐き気がします。

feel dizzy	*memai*	めまい
feel chilly	*samuke*	寒気
have a stomach ache	*fukustū*	腹痛
have a headache	*zutsū*	頭痛
have ringing ears	*miminari*	耳なり

I hurt myself.
Kega *o shimashita.*
けがをしました。

cut myself	*kirikizu*	切り傷
burned myself	*yakedo*	やけど
fell	*uchimi*	うちみ

I've been vomiting.
Zutto hakike ga shiteiru.
ずっと吐き気がしている。

Do you know what's wrong?
Doko ga okashi no desuka?
どこがおかしいのですか？

Is it serious?
Hidoi desuka?
ひどいですか？

Japanese dentists, like doctors, are acquainted with modern Western methods of care and treatment, although it may be more difficult to find one who speaks English.

Do you know a dentist who speaks English?
Eigo o hanasu haisha wa imasuka?
英語を話す歯医者はいますか？

Would you make an appointment for me?
Yoyaku o totte moraemasuka?
予約をとってもらえますか？

It hurts right here.
Koko ga itamu no desuga.
ここが痛むのですが。

I have a toothache.
Ha ga itai no desuga.
歯が痛いのですが。

My gums hurt.
Haguki ga itai no desuga.
歯ぐきが痛いのですが。

I've lost a filling.
Ha no tsumemono ga nakunarimashita.
歯のつめものがなくなりました。

Can you fix this?
Naorimasuka?
直りますか？

Traditional Japanese medicine is based on five millennia of Chinese medical practice, and you may have some opportunity to evaluate its effectiveness. Japan's *onsen*, the many hot springs that dot the volcanic Japanese islands, are also believed to have medicinal properties; the water of each is distinctive and efficacious for specific ailments.

Where can I get shiatsu?
Dokode shiatsu ga dekimasuka?
どこで指圧ができますか？

Where can I get accupuncture?
Dokode hari ga dekimasuka?
どこで針が出来ますか？

The problem is here.
Koko ga warui no desuga.
ここが悪いのですが。

How much is the charge per hour?
Ichijikan ikura desuka?
一時間いくらですか？

Can the acupuncturist come here?
Harishi o koko e yobemasuka?
針師をここへ呼べますか？

Can the shiatsu therapist come here?
Shiatsushi o koko e yobemasuka?
指圧師をここへ呼べますか？

I'd like to make an appointment.
Yoyaku o shitai no desuga.
予約をしたいのですが。

In addition to a full line of Western-style pharmaceuticals, Japanese pharmacies often stock concoctions based on *kanpō*, traditional Chinese medicine.

Where is a pharmacy?
Yakkyoku wa doko desuka?
薬局はどこですか？

I need some aspirin.
Asupirin o kudasai.
アスピリンをください。

adhesive tape	*bansoko*	絆創膏
band aids	*bando eido*	バンドエイド
cotton swabs	*menbō*	綿棒
condoms	*kondōmu*	コンドーム
cough drops	*kofu doroppu*	コフ・ドロップ
cough syrup	*kofu shiroppu*	コフ・シロップ
eye drops	*megusuri*	目薬
gauze	*gāze*	ガーゼ
insect repellent	*mushiyoke*	虫よけ
razor blades	*kamisori no ha*	カミソリの刃
sanitary napkins	*napukin*	ナプキン
tampons	*tanpon*	タンポン
toothpaste	*hamigakiko*	ハミガキ粉

Pharmacists may understand generic names (not trade names) of prescription drugs in English, but you must have a prescription — ask you doctor to please write neatly.

I need something for a cold.
Kazegusuri o kudasai.
かぜ薬をください。

cough	*sekidome*	咳どめ
headache	*chintsuzai*	鎮痛剤
stomach ache	*ichōyaku*	胃腸薬
indigestion	*shokazai*	消化剤
sore throat	*nodogusuri*	のど薬
constipation	*benpiyaku*	便秘薬
diarrhea	*geridome*	下痢止め

Can you fill this prescription?
Kono shohōsen dōri chōzai dekimasuka?
この処方箋どおり調剤できますか？

Which cold medicine do you recommend?
Dono kaze gusuri ga ii desuka?
この風邪薬がいいですか？

Besides being a resource in emergencies, the neighborhood police box, or *kōban*, is the place to report lost or found valuables, or just ask directions.

Please help me*!*
Tasukete kudasai!
助けてください！

Where is the police box?
Kōban wa doko desuka?
交番はどこですか？

Please call the police
Omawarisan *o yonde kudasai.*
おまわりさんを呼んでください。

an ambulance	*kyūkyūsha*	救急車
the fire department	*shōbōsho*	消防署
a tow truck	*rekkāsha*	レッカー車
a doctor	*isha*	医者

Please take me to the police.
Kōban *ni tsurete itte kudasai.*
交番につれていってください。

| a hospital | *byōin* | 病院 |
| a doctor | *isha* | 医者 |

An ambulance can be called by dialing the police emergency number, 110. Obviously, a medical emergency is not the time to be practicing your Japanese.

I've been robbed.
Gōtō ni aimashita.
強盗にあいました。

My wallet has been stolen.
Saifu o nusumaremashita.
サイフを盗まれました。

I've lost my wallet.
Saifu o otoshimashita.
サイフを落としました。

I want to report a fire!
Kaji da!
火事だ！

I want to report an accident!
Jiko da!
事故だ！

Someone is having a heart attack.
Shinzōmahi de taorete iru hito ga imasu.
心臓マヒでたおれている人がいます。

is choking	*nodo ni nanika tsumatta*
	のどに何かつまった
can't breathe	*kokyū konnan na*
	呼吸困難な
has had a accident	*jiko ni atta*
	事故にあった
has been hit by a car	*kōtsūjiko ni atta*
	交通事故にあった

Where Service Sells

There is no question but that in Japan services of all types are of the highest levels possible. Visitors are amazed by spotless, undented taxis, whose white-gloved drivers control automatic doors opening to seats draped with doilies, and who while away afternoon breaks cleaning their cars with feather dusters. Uniformed guards bow and politely direct passersby around spotless construction sites, apologizing for the inconvenience. For a real immersion into the wonderful excesses of Japanese service, stop in at a Japanese barber (p. 171) or gas station (p. 180).

• It often comes as a shock, therefore, to learn that this is country in which tipping is not a custom. There are exceptions — room maids in top-class Japanese inns, hired drivers (not taxis) — but the general rule is no tipping. The great service in Japan seems actually to come from the value placed on pleasing the customer and doing a job well, values which are drummed into new employees in militant training regimens that few Westerners would tolerate.

• There can be hidden costs for Japanese services, however. In addition to the three percent federal consumer tax added to all hotel and restaurant bills (often hidden in room and food prices), there is a three percent additional consumption tax on all restaurant checks over ¥7,500 and hotel tabs over ¥15,000, as well as a service charge of from ten to fifteen percent in fancy places (top-class hotels and hotel bars and restaurants). The key to keeping these costs down is obviously to have fewer services performed at posh places and to pay for them separately (don't charge your hotel restaurant tab to your room, for example).

• Regardless of your language ability, in Japan you can generally count on greater concern for your needs and interests than you might encounter elsewhere; you are a foreign visitor and therefore a guest. However, you must first capture the attention of a store clerk or salesperson, who may initially shy away from attending to you out of anxiety about the impending communication problem. For this reason, if you stay in Japan for any length of time, patronize your local mom-and-pop stores, whose family-owners will go out of their way to help you. Even better, have a Japanese neighbor introduce you.

• Getting services performed as you would like can be difficult anywhere, and the more particular you are, the more you should prepare. Use props, draw pictures, or get instructions written out in Japanese. And above all, be patient and watch. Japan is a place where the way of doing something is as important, sometimes more important, than the task itself.

For Further Information

The following organizations are referred to in *Fingertip Japanese* under related chapters. All telephone numbers are in Tokyo unless otherwise indicated. Dial area code 3 when calling a Tokyo number from outside the city.

Tourist Organizations

The Japan National Tourist Organization (JNTO) runs Tourist Information Centers (TIC) that provide brochures and travel information but do not assist with reservations. For this service you should visit an office of Japan Travel Bureau (JTB), a commercial tourist organization, or the travel desk at your hotel. They can help you make arrangements or reservations with any of the package tour operators, airlines, or associations listed below, or you may contact these organizations directly.

Japan National Tourist Organization	3216-1901
Tourist Information Center	
Tokyo	3502-1461
Narita Airport	(0476) 32-8711
Kyoto	(075) 371-5549
Japan Travel Bureau	
Foreign Tourist Division	3276-7777
Yokohama Branch	(045) 641-4111

If you are traveling in areas far from a TIC, you may get information (9 to 5 daily) via their toll-free Travel-Phone service:

For Eastern Japan	(0120) 222-800
For Western Japan	(0120) 444-800

Accommodations

Information may be obtained from the following organizations.

Japan Hotel Association	3279-2706
Japan Business Hotel Association	3258-1090
Japan Minshuku Association	3232-6561
Japan Ryokan Association	3231-5310
Japan Youth Hostel Association	3269-5831

Package Tour Operators

The following are listed in descending size of operating area.

Japan Travel Bureau (all areas)	3276-7777
Japan Amenity Travel (all areas)	3573-1011
Hankyu Express International (Kanto and Kansai)	3459-9080
Kinki Nippon Tourist (Kansai area)	3255-6535
Japan Gray Line (Tokyo)	3433-5745
Tobu Travel (Nikko)	3272-1806

Domestic Airlines

Any city in Japan can be reached by air from Tokyo in a few hours, by one or more of the following airlines.

Japan Air Lines	3552-6311
All Nippon Airways	3456-2111
Japan Air System	3438-1155

Japan Railpass

The following organizations can provide you with a voucher that can be exchanged for a railpass upon arrival in Japan. Numbers below are for the New York offices (area code 212) of these organizations; ask for the phone number and address of a branch office in your city.

Japan Air Lines	838-4400
Japan Travel Bureau	246-8030
Nippon Travel Agency	944-8660

Other Tourist Information

If you are in Japan but have not fixed your travel itinerary, the best place to start is at the Kokusai Kokan building and the Daimaru Department Store on the east side of Tokyo Station. These two buildings, which are close to each other, house the Tokyo branch offices of the tourists bureaus of all the main prefectures. Each prefecture has a separate office.

Ticket Agents

The following organizations can provide tickets to most events in the Kanto (Tokyo) area. Requests should be made in Japanese.

Ticket Pia	5237-9999
Classical music	5237-9990
Plays	5237-9988
Sports	5237-9977
Ticket Saison	5990-9999
Classical music	5990-9977

Call the following organizations for tickets in the Kansai (Kyoto, Nara, Osaka, Kobe) area:

Ticket Pia	(06) 363-9999
Ticket Saison	(06) 308-9999

Hospitals and Doctors (with English-speaking staff)

Tokyo
  St. Luke's International Hospital   3541-5151
Yokohama
  Bluff Clinic   (045) 641-6961
Osaka
  Yodogawa Christian Hospital   322-2250
Kyoto
  Japan Baptist Hospital   781-5194

Japan also has member clinics of IAMAT (International Association for Medical Assistance to Travelers), a worldwide organization offering a list approved English-speaking doctors and hospitals. To obtain a copy, write to 417 Center Street, Lewiston, N.Y. 14092, or 57 Voirets, 1212 Grand-Lancy, Geneva, Switzerland.

Lists of common items and expressions appear throughout the text under tasks for which they would obviously be useful. Their locations are also noted elsewhere in places where they would be useful to "customize" the sentences introduced. For example:

This book is interesting.   (ADJECTIVES, p. 84–85)
Kono hon wa omoshiroi desu.
この本はおもしろいです。

The "weathermark" indentifies this book as a production of Weatherhill, Inc., publishers of fine books on Asia and the Pacific. Typography, book, and cover design: Liz Trovato. Production supervision: Bill Rose. Typesetting: K-Kobo, New York, N.Y. Printing and binding: Daamen, Inc., West Rutland, Vermont. English text is set in Garamond; Japanese is set in Ryumin.